Praise for Past Work

Watercooler Wisdom

This book provides a roadmap for unleashing your energy and focusing it on what really matters most to you at work and home.

Tony Schwartz
Author of *The Power of Full Engagement* and
president of The Energy Project

An excellent book for anyone who wants to bring more consciousness into the way they work and improve their effectiveness and the way others respond to them.

Giles Bateman
Former chairman of CompUSA
and cofounder of Price Club

Watercooler Wisdom is an inspiring book that is both well researched and thoughtful. It provides excellent principles and practices that will engage you and show you how to transform the experience of stress in the workplace into personal satisfaction and prosperity. It's an essential companion for true success.

Lynne Twist
Author of *The Soul of Money*

This book provides a clever mirror to examine our internal thoughts and habits at work. It gives an opportunity for self-examination and advice that will be long valued by anyone who reads it.

Melba Pattillo Beals
Author of *Warriors Don't Cry* and
winner of the Congressional Gold Metal

Watercooler Wisdom shows us in a clear and simple way that we all have the ability to have a work life that runs like a fine Swiss watch.

Terry Jones
Founder of Travelocity

Watercooler Wisdom is an important read for anyone trying to get ahead in business or life. An insightful look at the best of human emotion at work.

Tom Latour
President of the Kimpton Hotel Group

This book gives important insight on how to thrive in today's rapidly changing business world and is a must read for aspiring young professionals or anyone wanting to have a successful career.

Stephen Seligman
Chief executive officer of The Learning Annex

This book provides the kind of guidance that ,when taken to heart, helps both seasoned workers and young people entering the work force develop excellent work habits for a lifetime of success and satisfaction.

Maddy Dychtwald
Cofounder of Age Wave and author of
Cycles: How We Will Live, Work, and Buy

Smart people will *love* this book. Like a series of brilliant coaching sessions, each tailored exactly to your personal needs, *Watercooler Wisdom* will put you on the positive side of things.

Raz Ingrasci
President and CEO of The Hoffman Foundation

60 Ways to Win Customers and
Keep Them Coming Back

Customer Service
In An Instant

- Master the four core customer styles
- Learn to say "no" with service
- Bounce back from service breakdowns

Keith Bailey & Karen Leland

CAREER
PRESS
Franklin Lakes, NJ

CUSTOMER SERVICE IN AN INSTANT
EDITED BY KATE HENCHES
TYPESET BY MICHAEL FITZGIBBON
Cover design by Howard Grossman/12e Design
Printed in the U.S.A. by Book-mart Press

To order this title, please call toll-free 1-800-CAREER-1 (NJ and Canada: 201-848-0310) to order using VISA or MasterCard, or for further information on books from Career Press.

CAREER
PRESS

The Career Press, Inc., 3 Tice Road, PO Box 687,
Franklin Lakes, NJ 07417
www.careerpress.com

Library of Congress Cataloging-in-Publication Data
Bailey, Keith, 1945-
    Customer service in an instant : 60 ways to win customers and keep them coming back / by Keith Bailey and Karen Leland.
    p. cm.
    Includes index.
    ISBN 978-1-60163-013-1
    1. Customer services. I. Leland, Karen. II. Title.

HF545.5.B3428 2008
658.8'12—dc22

                                                    2008013033

Acknowledgments

Deepest appreciation to our agent Matthew Carnicelli for believing in our idea for a series of business books, and finding them a most welcome home with Career Press. To Kristen Parkes and Michael Pye for guiding us through this process with flexibility. Lastly, to our spouses Jon Leland and Deborah Coffey—without their ongoing support no books would ever be possible and our lives would be considerably less.

Contents

Introduction

As most corporate giants and small businesses alike have realized, service—both online and off—is a critical concern for surviving and thriving in today's global, fast-paced, quick-changing, and high-tech business world. We are confident that *Customer Service In An Instant* will help you learn how to create and project a winning service attitude in the often stress-filled environment of work; discover powerful actions you can take to increase customer loyalty and retention, and apply time-tested techniques for dealing with difficult customers and coworkers.

Filled with real-world, practical advice gathered from Fortune 500 companies, small businesses, and entrepreneurs around the world, this book is for any manager or employee whose job involves frequent contact with external or internal customers by telephone, e-mail, or face-to-face. It will provide you with the essential skills you need to create the kind of service partnerships that lead to both satisfied customers and staff.

Assess Your Working Style

Your customer is a cautious type who craves facts and figures, your boss thrives on challenge and competition, and all you want is for everyone to just get along.

Service superstars understand that success means learning how to work with customers, coworkers, bosses, and vendors—many of whom have a different working style than their own.

Understanding the core working styles (and each one's attitude, approach, and expression) increases your ability to solve customer problems and decreases the amount of time it takes to get there. The place to start is by identifying your own individual working style.

Exercise:
How do you see yourself?

Consider each of the following attributes separately and assign a score to each one listed based on the following scale.

0 = Does not describe me at work.

1 = Describes me occasionally at work.

2 = Describes me a fair amount of the time at work.

3 = Describes me most of the time at work.

Keep in mind there are no right answers to these questions, so base your response on how you are today, not how you think you should be or would like to be in the future.

Customer Service In An Instant

_____ Achieving (A)

_____ Cooperative (C)

_____ Decisive (A)

_____ Deliberate (A)

_____ Diplomatic (C)

_____ Efficient (A)

_____ Enthusiastic (B)

_____ Factual (D)

_____ Friendly (C)

_____ Gregarious (B)

_____ Humorous (B)

_____ Independent (A)

_____ Intense (A)

_____ Lively (B)

_____ Logical (D)

_____ Organized (D)

_____ Outgoing (B)

_____ Patient (C)

_____ Persuasive (B)

_____ Relaxed (C)

_____ Reserved (D)

_____ Serious (D)

_____ Supportive (C)

_____ Systematic (D)

Now count up the total score for each of the letters A, B, C and D and write in your scores below:

My total A score is _____. A represents the Power Player.

My total B score is _____. B represents the Passionate Persuader.

My total C score is _____. C represents the People Pleaser.

My total D score is _____. D represent the Problem Solver.

Research in the field of individual styles goes as far back as a Greek medical philosopher in the Roman Empire named Claudius Galen who developed a theory of personality based on the four humors. Since then, many famous researchers, consultants, and psychiatrists (chief among them Carl Jung) have studied and further developed the concept. One thing many agree on is that these styles measure two important aspects of a person's behavior:

1. **Assertiveness:** This is expressed as confidence in the way you state your opinion, idea, position or claim, and the willingness to be strong and forceful as needed.

2. **Emotional Expression:** This is expressed as easily and strongly showing a great deal of feeling and emotion.

Each of the four core working styles has a different level of assertiveness and emotional expression.

The Four Core Working Styles

1. **The Power Player (your A score):** Power Players have a high degree of assertiveness but a lower degree of emotional expression

2. **The Passionate Persuader (your B score):** Passionate Persuaders have a high degree of both assertiveness and emotional expression

3. **The People Pleaser (your C score):** People Pleasers have a high degree of emotional expression but a lower degree of assertiveness

4. **The Problem Solver (your D score):** Problem Solvers have a low degree of both emotional expression and assertiveness.

Your primary working style describes the most common approach you take in dealing with people and situations at work. Although everyone tends to have a smattering of each style within them, usually one or two working styles act as your default position. The style in which you scored the most points is likely to be your primary working style.

If you have two scores that are the same or very close together, you can figure out your more dominant one by reading the specific descriptions for each style later in this book. If you're still stumped then ask a coworker to fill out the questionnaire—they can usually peg you on the spot.

Lastly, don't fall into the trap of thinking that one style is better than another. Everyone expresses him- or herself differently, and each style adds to the diversity of the workplace.

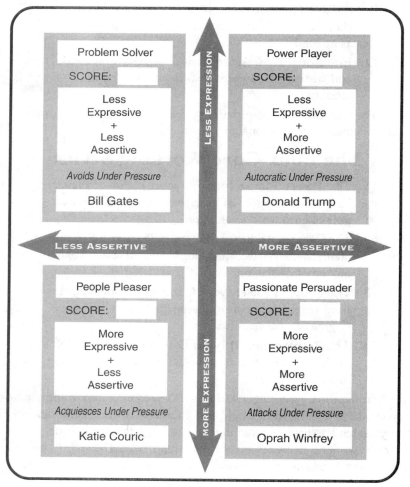

Avoid Negative Filters

Stupid, jerk, lazy, liar, pushy, crazy, and crabby—negative names you call customers in the privacy of your own mind, or occasionally out loud to a coworker.

Negative filters get their start in life when you pin a not-so-nice label on a difficult customer. For example, you might decide that a customer, who keeps asking what seem to be obvious questions, is "stupid."

Having a negative filter is like wearing rose-colored glasses. The difference is that negative filters don't paint a rosy picture, just the opposite; they foster a critical and unhelpful attitude that begins a downward spiral from which it can be hard to recover.

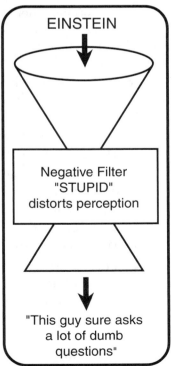

Once you have a negative filter in place, it distorts your perception. Your customer might be the next Einstein, but if you've decided they're "stupid," everything they do and say becomes evidence of how dumb they are.

Consider this conversation between a customer and an associate (with a "stupid" negative filter) at a large, office supply warehouse:

Customer Service In An Instant

Customer: *"Excuse me, I'm looking for a small drafting board."*

Associate: *"They're on aisle four."*

A few moments later...

Customer: *"I looked on aisle four and I can't see them."*

Associate: *(huffing)* *"Well that's where they are. They're big—I don't see how you could miss them."*

Customer: *"Could you show me?"*

Associate: *"Well, they are definitely there...okay (begrudgingly), I'll take you there."*

Being a professional the associate knows better than to come right out and say, "Hey, lady, you're not too bright, are you?" but the negative filter "stupid" still comes through, loud and clear.

Negative filters click into place when customers behave in a way that reminds you of a particular filter. For example what are some of the specific actions that you associate with a "pushy" filter? They might include: Not following instructions, demanding to see a supervisor, not taking no for an answer, or asking the same question over and over.

Remember there are many reasons why customers act as they do. For example a customer may ask the same question over and over again because:

- Your explanation was unclear.
- They got distracted and stopped listening.
- They didn't like the answer and hoped for a different one.
- Their spouse was sick at home and they were worried.
- Their dog just died.

Regardless, viewing them through a filter, instead of addressing their needs, leads to lost time, wasted energy and increased irritation on both parties parts.

2

Exercise:

Below is a common negative filter(a few common ones we can't put in print). Take a moment and write down what observable behaviors you would expect to see for this filter.

Negative Filter: Rude

Example: When a customer doesn't listen to what I m saying.

Look at the behaviors you wrote down and now ask yourself what other reasons there might be for the customer behaving that way:

_____

_____

_____

Example: A customer may not listen to what I am saying because they are upset or concerned.

_____

_____

_____

Inevitably, you will have negative filters about some of your customers, some of the time, but you always have a choice about whether you are going to focus on them. The trick is to avoid getting stuck in Negative Filters and switch to a Service Filter.

Backtrack Key Words

No matter how focused and attentive you are, it's easy to misinterpret what a customer is saying. Backtracking helps reduce the gap between what the customer says and what you hear. By repeating to the customer, in your own words, what they have just said to you, you give them the opportunity to correct anything that you misheard and ensure that you are both on the same page.

For example, the customer gives you a long explanation such as, "I have a variable mortgage and I'm thinking that I might be better off refinancing and switching to a fixed—although the last time I inquired the fixed rates were a lot more expensive."

Rather than repeat back parrot fashion what the customer has just said, backtrack by saying, "So you are wondering whether to switch to a fixed mortgage—if the difference in monthly payments isn't too much?"

Besides backtracking whole phrases, you can also backtrack key words. When customers hear these words repeated, they feel that they are talking to a person who understands them and a more collaborative conversation takes place.

For example, if the customer says, "The last time I called in I was told that there were a handful of viable options available to me. That was a month ago, have rates changed enormously since then?"

Words such as "handful," "viable," "options," and "enormously" all stand out as unique to this customer's way of describing their situation. The service provider can now backtrack some of these keywords by saying to the customer, "Let me look and see what viable options are currently available."

Exercise:

Review each of the following customer statements and list the keywords that you would backtrack if you were talking to this customer.

1. "Whenever I call in to place an order I am put on hold for an inordinate amount of time. Are you short on staff?"

2. "I bought these shoes last week, and they squish my toes. Do you have them half-a-size up?"

3. "Can I get the magazine subscription for a month, on a tentative basis, see if I like the read, and if I don't, cancel it for a reimbursement?"

4. "Can the help desk get this fixed ASAP or am I going to forego the use of my equipment for the rest of the day?"

Answers:
1. Inordinate and short. 2. Squish and half-a-size
3. Tentative, cancel, and Reimbursement.
4. ASAP, Forego, Rest of the day

Be Web Wise

The Web offers a great option to better serve your customers, but, used poorly, can backfire and create distance instead of the closeness you had desired. To ensure that your Website woos without woe:

Make Your Site Easy to Navigate

Customers who get frustrated because they can't navigate your site with ease will leave. The brave new frontier of cyberspace has brought with it the expectation that it should take no longer than a nanosecond to move from page to page.

Confusing, awkwardly designed, and poorly labeled sites are a major cause of customer frustration. You can make your site navigation more customer-friendly by:

- Providing a short description under any links, so that visitors understand to what page they will be connected.

- Placing main navigation buttons together on the page, rather than spreading them out. This makes them easier to find and use.

- Clearly and logically naming the sections of your site, so that they are easy to understand. In addition, highlight the section of the site that is currently being explored, so customers know where they are located.

Offer Alternative Contact Options

A recent trend in Website design is omitting company phone numbers or burying them so deeply that they are impossible to find (the thinking being that e-mail is less expensive than having to answer the phone). But sometimes only a phone call will do, and then the potential of alienating a customer can cost your company dearly. The bottom line is, do business with your customers the way they want to do business with you. This means listing all contact information, including phone, fax, street address, and e-mail on your site.

Provide Speedy Downloads

Most customers start getting antsy if a download takes longer than 10 seconds. If your site provides this type of material, be sure that it doesn't take forever for customers to receive it. The usual suspects for slow downloads are:

- Inadequately compressed photographs and images.
- Animated and overly fussy graphics.
- Over-complicated page layouts and text effects such as an overabundance of drop shadows.

Keep It Simple

It can be tempting to use all the bells and whistles that Web design can provide but doing so looks unprofessional and confusing. Customers like a site that clearly provides the information for which they are looking—without confusing backgrounds, spinning animations, undecipherable fonts, and ugly graphics.

It's always a good idea to have a few users, who are unfamiliar with your site, visit and report back any problems they encounter or ideas for improvement.

Provide FAQs

Many customers who visit your site have questions that you have answered a thousand times before. Offering an FAQ (Frequently Asked Questions) section allows customers to search for an answer from your cataloged list without you having to respond to the same inquiry over and over. FAQs work well as long as you provide alternatives for getting answers to questions not found in the FAQ list.

What's in a Name?

Keep in mind that the first contact your customers have with your company may be your domain name popping up after a Google search. The domain name you choose creates a first impression and can make it easy (or hard) for potential customers to find your company in the first place. The Web Wise know that the most successful domain names are:

- Easy to remember.
- Easy to understand.
- Relevant to your current business.
- Easy for people to spell and pronounce.
- Not being used by someone else.
- Doesn't resemble, too closely, another company's domain name.

Customer Service In An Instant

Because buying, creating, and selling domain names has become big business, it's now a bit harder to come up with an original URL or even find one that is available. To pick a winner try the following:

1. Brainstorm key words. What words represent your company name and the product or service you offer? What words represent the values and/or qualities you stand for? What words represent your customers buying criteria?

2. Select key words. After you've filled up a few flip chart pages with potential words ask yourself – how do these words feel? How do they sound? Narrow down the list and pick three to six key words you might build your domain name around.

3. Put it together. Try mixing and matching the words you've chosen into various combinations that may work. Because many domain names are already spoken for, a few tricks to try to make yours more available include:

   - Use a name you like and make it plural.
   - Add a hyphen.
   - Put a word in front of your keyword such as: The, About, My, Get, Find, Your, and so on.
   - Place a word behind your keyword such as Place, Shop, Deals, Info, Central, Zone, and so on.
   - Add geography by tacking your location onto the front or back of the key words.

4. Pick a domain name that travels well: The proliferation of the Web has made it possible even for small businesses and entrepreneurs to market their wares around the world! While some names work like a charm in the United States, due to cultural differences and translation, these same names may be a disaster in another country.

Just for Good Measure

If you already have a Website up and running and are not getting the response you want, consider the following areas where updates or changes may be needed:

- When compared to your competitors, how does your site hold up?
- Are you currently well positioned in the search engines so that potential clients can easily find you?
- Do you need to freshen up your content to encourage people to come back?
- Is your contact information easily found on your homepage?
- Are you maximizing the use of metatags on all pages?
- Have you included too much information on a page, making it crowded and hard to read?
- Do you provide visitors something for free on you site?
- Can you do something to make your site more interactive?
- Are you collecting the e-mail addresses of your visitors, so that you can contact them?
- Do you have an e-newsletter to which your visitors can subscribe?
- Are all your links currently up and working?
- Do you accept credit cards online, making it easy for customers to buy right away?

Beware of Burnout

Numerous studies show that jobs (such as customer service and technical support) that involve dealing with customer complaints on a daily basis are among the most stressful. Recent surveys by ComPsych Corporation show that 63 percent of U.S. workers are "stressed to the point of feeling extremely fatigued and out of control." This kind of stress is the result of constant pressure, mental exhaustion, and physical strain, and, unchecked, it can lead to burn-out. Burnout is the feeling of being completely drained with nothing more to give. Symptoms can include feeling:

- Powerless
- Hopeless
- Emotionally exhausted
- Isolated
- Irritable
- Frustrated
- Trapped

Burnout doesn't hit all at once, but gets slowly worse through time and follows four distinct phases.

1. Exhaustion

You are overwhelmed. You have too much to do in too little time. Your schedule is out of control so you start cutting corners and doing work that doesn't measure up to your normal standard of excellence. Arriving home, you are so physically and mentally drained that all you can do is plop down in front of the T.V. with a gallon of ice cream and zone out until its time to go to bed. If not arrested at this point, you move into a state of uncertainty.

2. Uncertainty

Because sheer exhaustion has you cutting corners, you start to believe (inaccurately) that you are an imposter, and not the reliable worker and colleague others think you are. You just can't hold it all together anymore and feelings of uncertainty and guilt descend. You bring vulnerability and insecurity home with you and constantly wonder if family and friends notice that under the thin veneer of "everything's great," things are really falling apart. Not surprisingly many people deal with this phase by creating a heavy layer of armor, which leads to an abrasive exterior.

5

3. Abrasiveness

Scared to show what's really going underneath, you keep friends, family, and colleagues at arm's length with a sarcastic and cynical attitude. A prickly demeanor insures that coworkers go out of their way to avoid you. Short term, this strategy works because you isolate yourself from others and don't have to deal with your feelings of insecurity. Long term, this strategy is doomed to failure because your abrasive shell separates you from the very people who could support you in escaping from burnout's downward spiral.

4. Failure

By the time you get to this phase all your inner defenses have worn down. Your body armor is showing signs of wear and your inner turmoil is beginning to leak out all over the place. You become ultra-sensitive and innocent remarks from colleagues at work can cause you to take offense and overreact angrily.

If any of these descriptions make you sit up and say, "Hey—that's me!" seek help. Don't try and "muscle through" to prove that you are not a wimp. Burnout can have serious consequences—physical, emotional, and spiritual. Seek out your Human Resources Department or Employee Assistance Program.

Stress Versus Burnout

While everyday stress and even occasional intense stress is an expected part of work life, burnout is a whole different animal.

Stress causes you to overreact emotionally.		Burnout causes you to shut down your emotions.
Stress makes everything seem urgent.	**vs.**	Burnout makes everything seem unimportant.
Stress drains your energy.		Burnout kills your motivation and hope.
Stress leads to over activity.		Burnout leads to listlessness.

9

Bridge the Language Barrier

Your customer is calling from Italy, your boss made his way to the Boston office by way of Beijing, your coworker in the next cubicle hails from China, and you grew up in Topeka, Kansas. In an ever-shrinking world, going global can mean dealing with more and more people whose native language is different from your own. Misunderstandings are easy enough when your are speaking the same language, so you have to be doubly diligent when an accent is part of the mix. Below are some guidelines to help you bridge the language barrier and successfully deal with customers from other countries and cultures.

Rephrase, Don't Shout

This is an easy trap to fall into. The customer doesn't understand you the first time so you raise your voice and repeat what you just said. They still don't get it, so you speak even louder and on it goes. Instead of saying the same thing over again try using different words and phrases until your message has been understood.

Say "I Don't Understand"

Don't say okay, act as if you understand what's being said and then go along with the conversation, when you really don't. Providing stellar service is impossible if you have no idea what the customer is talking about. Yes, it's embarrassing, but it won't cause an international incident for you to explain that you are having some difficulty understanding them. You can always ask your customer to slow down a little and then repeat back to them, what you heard.

Take It Slow

Resist the urge to avoid dealing with a hard-to-understand accent by making a 100-yard-dash to the end of the conversation. Instead, speak more slowly than usual and give the customer extra time to respond. Remember, this person may be having just as a hard a time understanding your accent as you are understanding his.

Brush Up Your Language Skills

If you deal with one population of foreign speakers more than another, keep a few handy sentences posted near your desk. Service providers often find themselves using the same phrases over and over, and knowing how to say them in another language is a useful tool.

Practice Polite

Your attitude is communicated less by the words you use and more by your tone of voice. Maintaining a polite stance and presenting a happy-to-help tone crosses the international divide and is welcomed in any language.

Build a Bridge

Bridging is a technique our clients love to pull out of their toolboxes when faced with verbose customers. It's a great way to politely get a customer or co-worker back on track after they have veered off point.

Below is a recreation of a conversation between a passenger booking an airline ticket and the reservation agent:

Customer Service In An Instant

Keith: *"...I need a flight to Dallas, please."*

Agent: *"What date are you leaving?"*

Keith: *"The client wants me to start work on April 19th, so I need to leave on April 18th."*

Agent: *"Okay. Do you prefer a morning or afternoon flight?"*

Keith: *"Morning. Oh, wait, that's my wife's birthday...I forgot that when I set up the meeting...I was out-of-town for her birthday last year...Problem is this is the only date that works for the client and they have a lot of people coming from out of town for the meeting. This is terrible. I also promised my wife that we would go out for her birthday...she's going to be really upset..."*

Agent: *"I can see your difficulty. There are still plenty of seats left on this flight, so do you want to work it out and call back or should I look at the red eye flights?"*

Keith: *"Okay. I'll talk to my wife and call back. Thanks."*

The agent (for Delta Airlines—let's give credit where credit is due) did a perfect job of politely curtailing Keith's ramblings and getting the conversation back on track. Keith was wrapped up in his dilemma but the agent used the bridging technique to cut to the chase and build a bridge between what Keith was saying and where the agent wanted the interaction to go.

The first part of bridging is waiting for the customer to take a breath. They all breathe eventually, so it's a matter of waiting for an entry point.

The second part is quickly slipping in an emphatic phrase. The agent interrupted with "I can see your difficulty." This empathetic phrase softened the interruption and kept it from sounding rude or abrupt.

Lastly, use a close-ended question to get to where you want to be. The agent bridged back by saying, "Do you want to work it out and call back?" This brought Keith to his senses and prompted a short answer that saved time for both parties.

Choose Your Level of Conversation

One quick conversation with a coworker, internal customer or your boss about a situation does not always bring about the changes you had hoped for. By the same token, it's pointless to keep having the same conversation over and over when it isn't making any difference. To deal with a persistent issue begin at level one and if necessary work your way through to level three. Good Luck!

Level One: The Basic Issue

In this first conversation you lay out the problem from your perspective, and you listen to your coworkers take on the issue. The objective is to come up with actions or solutions you mutually agree upon. For example:

Deborah: *"The last few months, your information for the sales report was turned in late. I'm concerned about this and am counting on you to get it in on time this month. Can you do that?"*

Ty: *"Sorry about that. I've been really busy working on the Shipman account. I will get it in on time this month."*

Level Two: New Strategies

If the issue is not resolved at level one, level two focuses on the recurring pattern, the underlying reasons why things are not happening, and what measures can be taken to remedy the situation.

Deborah: *"I was expecting your sales information in on time this month. It was late again, and that really put my team in*

> *a bad situation. This is the third month in a row that it's been late, even though you said it wouldn't be. Why are you having a problem with this?"*

Ty: *"I'm so sorry. I know I said I would have it to you on time, but I am still stuck on the Shipman account. I guess I'm just not able to fit it in."*

Deborah: *"I appreciate that, but things can't go on this way. The sales report needs to be in on time. What specifically can you do to fit it in and make sure it gets to me on time?"*

Ty: *"I know I need to make it a priority. I could put it in my schedule to work on Friday afternoons when things are bit slower."*

Level Three: An Issue of Trust

If the problem has not been resolved by the prior conversations, it's time to have a talk that goes beyond the specific issue to how this situation is affecting your relationship. You may find that you are beginning to doubt what your coworker says, losing trust in them and feeling as if they don't respect your time and energy. It can be uncomfortable and challenging to bring these things up, but it's necessary if you want to resolve the issue long term and maintain a good working relationship.

Deborah: *"Ty, I was really upset that your sales information was not in on time this month. Given our past two conversations and your promise to do it on Friday afternoons, I was surprised. At this point, I feel like I can't count on you."*

Ty: *"I know, I know. I tried my best, but I just didn't seem to get to it."*

Deborah: *"I hear that but this is starting to affect my relationship with you. I don't trust you to do what you say you are going to do. That feels really bad to me. I want to know that I can depend on you."*

Ty: *"I feel really bad about that, but I don't know what to do. The Shipman account is my priority right now."*

Deborah: *"I appreciate that, but do you think that is worth jeopardizing our working relationship over this? I can't believe there isn't a way to work this out."*

Ty: *"I'm really sorry, I had no idea this was having that much of an impact. I will work on the sales report on Fridays, and I will send you a e-mail with the status, every week."*

Sadly, not all conversations that make their way to level three will be resolved on the first go round (or ever), but the chances of resolution are greater if you continue to communicate about the real feelings and issue goings on, and not just the circumstances surrounding them.

Conquer Complaining Customers

Your customers supply some of the best feedback about what needs to be changed in your company policy, procedure, and product. Every business receives these complaints; the smart ones view them as a source of valuable information. It's easy to get defensive and miss these hidden gems if you don't know how to identify and deal with customer complaint styles.

The Go-for-the-Throaters

These customers are angry and in-your-face (or in-your-ear on the phone). Their complaints are loud, lengthy, and involved. You can barely get a word in edgewise.

Respond by staying quiet. Try not to interrupt. Instead, let them spin out their story and, from time to time, say uh huh, okay, and I follow you. Once they have burned through their emotions, use closed-ended questions to quickly gather any additional information you need. Let them know you appreciate their feedback and what you plan on doing about it.

The Quiet-as-a-Mousers

These customers have a problem but don't speak up about it. Their complaints come in the form of little clues you pick up in their tone of voice or body language. They may not say anything negative, but you can tell they're dissatisfied. It's tempting to ignore the signs and pretend that everything is okay, but, remember, an unhappy customer is likely to tell other people how he or she feels.

Respond by digging a little deeper. Check to see what's going on by asking a leading question such as, "Was the service/product what you expected?" A curious question, asked sincerely, can get even the quietest of customers to open up and reveal their problems.

The High Rollers

These customers have high standards and will settle for nothing but perfection. They are willing to pay for the gold standard of service, and, if they don't get it, will let you know in a no-nonsense manner.

Respond by energetically and enthusiastically gathering all the information you need to fix the problem—then, fix it! These customers are interested in solid results delivered in a speedy way—not excuses.

The Whiners

These customers seem to make a profession of complaining. Yes, they call you every month; yes, they are never happy; yes, you are tired of hearing their voice; yes, you want to ignore them, but they are not going away just because you wish they would.

Respond by switching to a Service Filter (see way 51) and mustering all the patience you can summon. Listen to what they are saying, don't argue, apologize, and ask questions that show interest and concern (yes, it's hard). Most whiners are placated when they know you are interested and will do whatever you can to fix the issue.

The Tricksters

These customers complain as a strategy to get something for nothing. No matter what you say, do, or offer, it's not good enough. Their goal is to escalate the situation until they can get something from you, that they are not entitled to or is not fair given the circumstances.

Respond by checking the facts and making sure they support your suspicion. If they do, stay firm and only offer what is fair and reasonable under your company guidelines. Don't be derogatory or make accusations—no matter how transparent their motivation.

Counter Coworker Conflict

Getting along with coworkers isn't always easy, but it is downright difficult when they act in ways that are immature, irresponsible, or irritating. Trying to stop your coworkers from ever being angry or upset is a no-win battle. But keeping your own natural reactions in check can be done if you have an idea of the dynamics at play. Here are three common coworker conflict situations and what to do about them.

Escalating Out of Control

A coworker makes a remark that you don't like, and you up the ante by coming back with a snappy, even more disrespectful reply. Your coworker takes offense and does the same back to you—only one better—and you're off! Before you know it, voices are raised, tempers are hot, and the conversation is spiraling out of control.

What to do about it

Let your coworker have the last word. If you can drop your defensive posture, you will be able to listen to his or her point of view, discuss it, and then present your ideas or opinions.

Stay quiet for five seconds before you respond to what your coworker has said. A moment of silence gives you the time you need to stop from zinging back with an automatic, negative response.

Pace your coworker to let him/her know that you are listening and appreciate their perspective—even though you may disagree.

Smoothing Things Over

Your coworker is upset with you, but pretends that nothing is wrong and that no conflict exists. When you try to talk with them about the situation, they smooth things over by saying "everything's fine." Like it or not, the conflict will bubble to the surface one way or another, often when you least expect it.

What to do about it

Ask your coworker specific, detailed questions about what's going on and don't settle for vague answers and feel good platitudes.

Keep your tone soft and avoid language that makes it sound as if you are accusing the other person. When a coworker is holding something back, he or she is probably doing so to avoid conflict, not because he/she is dishonest.

Don't overreact. Assuming that the other person hasn't done something really bad (like steal your client), most conflicts can be resolved by patiently pursuing simple communication.

Serving Up Put-Downs

Your coworker believes that something unfair has happened to him/her but doesn't talk to you directly about it. The unresolved and unspoken feelings slowly turn to resentment. Your coworker indirectly expresses this resentment by implicitly putting down your feelings, opinions, and ideas.

What to do about it

Don't try and defend yourself against your coworker's comments—they're really a smoke screen covering a deeper issue. Try to listen for the message underneath. You can get to the cause of the underlying resentment by asking what, if anything, you may have done (or not done) that has upset them.

Don't Get Aggressive—Get Assertive

If you're unsure about how to strike that delicate balance between straightforward communication and in your face fervor, you may unintentionally create conflict between yourself and your coworkers. By flying off the handle and becoming aggressive, you force those around you into a defensive posture that makes hearing what you have to say (no matter how wise and well thought out) hard to hear. The following tips will help you assert your thoughts, feelings, and opinions in a non-threatening way.

Talk about actions. Make sure that you describe the situation in as specific terms as possible. For example, saying "You don't communicate well," is going to create more conflict than saying, "You did not call me today, like you said you would."

Stick to what you can see. Avoid the temptation to read your coworker's mind and assign meaning and motives for why they did what they did. Making inaccurate statements about the inspirations behind your coworker's actions will make them defensive. Instead try to describe only what is observable. For example, saying "You felt so guilty, you couldn't even talk to me," won't work as well as saying, "After I spoke with you, you did not say hello to me for a week."

Steer clear of generalizations. When describing the other person's behavior avoid qualifiers such as *always* and *never*. For example, "You never step in and man the phones when the help desk gets backed up." Instead, focus on a specific incident. For example, "You did not offer to man the phones this week, when the help desk backed up."

Stay steady. Pacing back and forth, tugging at your hair or clothes, twirling a pen and so on, are all nervous habits that will diminish the power of what you are saying. Instead, look your coworker directly in the eye (being careful not to stare them down) and confidently say what you mean, and mean what you say.

Create Customer-Friendly Systems

Many managers scratch their heads in confusion when considering how to make their policies, procedures, and technology (systems) more customers-friendly. Systems, while necessary, can be your customer's best friend or worst enemy, depending on how they are designed. The two principal problems are:

1. Systems whose aim is to protect the company from employees or customers taking advantage of them. For example: The delivery procedure for a large manufacturer required delivery personnel to call the distribution center for authorization on returns. The call was then routed to the warehouse manager who, in turn, called the sales manager for approval, and so on. This time and energy consuming procedure delayed the driver and consequently made him late for his next delivery. This inefficiency was further compounded by the fact that permission to return the merchandise was granted in 90 percent of the cases.

2. Systems that are part of how a company has *always* done business and no one questions their validity or effectiveness.

As one observant manager said, "'In our company, adhering to the procedures and policies overrides common sense."

Although there are endless systems that may need an overhaul within your company, the most important ones to review and revise include:

- Sales/ordering systems.
- Supply/logistics systems.
- Accounting/payment systems.
- After sales service systems.
- Complaint procedures.
- Crisis/contingency systems.
- Telephone/computer systems.

Examining and changing in-focused systems (those that work favorably for the company but unfavorably for the customer) is essential to a successful service improvement process.

Thought Starters

1. Do we look for ways to simplify procedures and reduce bureaucracy so that the customer may be better served?
2. Do we use customer feedback to make changes to our systems and procedures?
3. Do we have the computer technology in place to provide our customers with quality service?
4. Do we have adequate telephone systems to provide quality service to customers?
5. Do we use employee feedback to update or change in-focused systems?

Define Customer Needs

Imagine you go into a store to buy a toaster oven. As you make your way back to the car, toaster oven firmly in your grasp you find yourself thinking, "That was really great service." What was it that made it great?

- Friendliness
- Understanding and empathy
- Fairness
- Control
- Reliability
- Expertise
- Easy to do business with
- Professional

Now, imagine you go into that same store for a toaster oven, and they don't have it in stock. As you are walking back to your car, empty handed, you're thinking, "That was great service!" When you don't get exactly what you need or want as a customer and you still get good service, what are some of the additional qualities that are important to you?

- Options
- Empathy
- Apology
- Information

If you hold the common misconception that service is *only* giving customers what they ask for, you paint yourself into a corner. If, on the other hand, you expand your definition of service to include the multitude of less obvious, and unspoken, customer needs—such as being helpful and courteous—you will never encounter a time when you can't provide your customers with some level of service. Focusing on these unspoken needs is particularly useful when you cannot say yes to a customer request because of regulations, policies, contractual limitations, back-orders, out-of-stock items, and so on.

Regardless, the heart of providing service is asking yourself the question:

"What does this person need, and how can I provide it to the best of my ability?"

Because different customers have different needs and because even the same customer has different needs at different times, it's important that you always ask yourself this question.

A Multitude of Needs

Which of the following needs are the most important to your customers?

accessible	dependable	knowledgeable
accurate	discreet	leading-edge
attentive	easy to do business with	low cost
attractive	easy to locate	personal
authentic	easy to use	private
available	effective	professional
careful	efficient	quick
caring	entertaining	reliable
clean	exciting	responsible
comfortable	experienced	responsive
competitive	fair	safe
consistent	fast	skilled
convenient	flexible	trustworthy
cost-effective	healthy	understanding
courteous	helpful	unique
creative	honest	up-scale
customized	innovative	well-known
dedicated	interesting	well-stocked

Deliver Constructive Criticism

Most people don't relish the idea of receiving negative feedback, and they like giving it even less. The next time you have a criticism to communicate to a coworker, boss, or customer, keep the following in mind:

Don't communicate when angry. Do get calm before you speak. Criticizing someone else's actions when you are angry or upset often leads to polarization and argument. You take your offensive stand, the other person reacts and gets defensive, you get even more upset that they are not hearing you, they dig their heels in and you're off to the races. The opportunity to communicate is lost.

Don't hide statements behind questions. Do be direct. Often, to avoid the discomfort of making a straightforward communication, people hide their criticism, behind a question: "Bob, are you having a problem getting to work on time?" A better approach would be for the speaker to be straightforward "Bob, I am concerned with the number of times you have been late to work this week."

Don't discuss everything at once. Do focus on one point at a time. You may have a list of 10 things that bug you about Sally from Sales, but trying to talk to her about all of them at the same time won't get you very far. As the expression goes "choose your battles." Most people can only handle one clearly defined criticism at a time.

Don't label. Do be specific. Don't make your point by putting a negative label on the other person: "Bob, you are just lazy." This puts the other person on the defensive and almost guarantees that they will tune out any legitimate criticism you have. A better strategy is to tell the other person exactly what behavior(s) you have observed and why you find them objectionable. The more judicious and less judgmental you are in your comments, the better chance you have of getting your point across.

Don't confront people in public. Do pick a private place. No one likes getting negative feedback in front of other people. Meetings, conference calls, and break rooms are generally the wrong place to make your feelings known. Instead, pick a quiet spot (such as a conference room or private office) where you can have a one on one discussion.

Don't just criticize. Do reaffirm your confidence in the other person. It's all to easy to just put forth the negative and leave out the positive. Always end any criticism by reaffirming you faith and trust in the other person's ability to handle the situation, make the correction, or resolve the problem.

Feedback Cheat Sheet

Step One: Describe the situation as you see it with as much specific detail as possible.

Laurie, your customer satisfaction scores have been below average for the past few months. I've listened to you on the phone, and lately I've noticed you being a bit short with customers. I am concerned about this.

Step Two: Ask the person for their perspective or understanding on what you said.

Do you feel like you have been short with customers? Why do you think your scores are below average?

Step Three: Come to a mutual understanding of each other's point of view and work out any misunderstandings. .

Laurie, I understand that stress at home is making you a bit short-tempered at work, but I hope you can understand my point. You can't take that out on our customers.

Step Four: Agree to a plan of action.

We agree that you are going to register for the company stress reduction class and make sure to take your full lunch break every day. Right?

Step Five: Follow up and recognize any improvement.

Laurie, I really noticed how much of an effort you have been making to be patient with customers. I appreciate your taking the feedback seriously.

Ditch Your Default Response

Part of the art of customer service is negotiating sticky situations by avoiding tricky turns of phrase that can land the service provider in hot water and make the customer's blood boil. To avoid making an already difficult situation worse, avoid the following phrases and try out these customer friendly alternatives.

You need to calm down.

Switch to: "I understand why you are upset and let's see what we can do to resolve this situation."

A customer service representative telling an upset adult to calm down is the equivalent of a fireman throwing gasoline onto a house fire. If you want your customers to go from hot to cold, empathize with their plight, apologize if appropriate, and let them know that you are on their side in finding a solution to the problem.

That's not my department.

Switch to: "The quickest way to get this taken care of is to speak with..."

From time to time customers may ask you to resolve a problem or deal with a situation that is not within your scope of authority to handle. In this case, your job is to become the catalyst for getting that customer to the right person and the right place to help solve their problem.

I can't do that.

Switch to: "What I can do is..." or "What you can do is..."

Customers don't like to hear that they can't have what they want, when they want it, but most do understand that there are limits to what the service provider is able to do. Instead of focusing on the negative and what you can't do, try offering options about what you can do and what the customer can do to get the satisfaction they desire.

It's not my fault.

Switch to: "I am going to help you solve this."

There is an old adage that goes "fix the problem, not the blame." When an angry customer starts accusing you of creating a problem, the natural reaction is to become defensive and proclaim your innocence. However, if you can avoid letting a defensive reaction rule the day and instead set your sites on problem resolution, you will satisfy the customer faster and with less stress.

I'm busy right now.

Switch to: "Thanks for waiting, I'll be with you as soon as I can."

When you're in the middle of serving one customer, stopping dead in your tracks and assisting another one (who is fidgeting impatiently) is not an easy situation. Some service people handle this by tossing out a curt, "I'm busy right now" which is their way of saying, "Why are you bothering me, can't you see I'm busy?" A better approach is to let the customer know you see them and will get to them ASAP.

You need to talk to my manager.

Switch to: "I can help you."

Customers sometimes ask you for things that are a little outside of company policy or procedure. At such times, quickly passing them off to your manager is tempting. Instead, focus on what you can do to help them. If your manager does need to be involved, take the initiative to go to him or her, yourself, and return to the customer with a solution in hand. Doing so makes you the service hero in the customers' eyes.

You want it by when?

Switch to: "I'll try my best."

When customers make demands by asking you for something that is unreasonable and difficult to provide, your first reaction may be annoyance. However, because you have little control over your customers' requests, the best approach is to hold off on any negative judgments and try your best to accommodate the requests. Never promise something with only the hope that you can deliver. Giving customers unrealistic expectations may get them off your back in the short term, but it will blow up in your face later. Do make promises that you know you can accomplish and assure customers, with confidence and enthusiasm, that you know how important their deadlines are and that you'll try your best to meet them.

Evaluate Your Service Skills

The following questionnaire will help you objectively assess your service strengths and challenges. Please rate each question according to this scale:

0 = Rarely

1 = Sometimes

2 = Often

3 = Almost Always

1. Rather than focus on my own convenience, I usually do things for the convenience of the customer. _____

2. I make myself readily available to help customers rather than avoiding them. _____

3. I use eye contact when speaking with customers to show attentiveness. _____

4. I pace the customer by adjusting my inflection, rate of speech, and volume as appropriate. _____

5. I ask appropriate questions and actively gather important facts in order to solve a customer's problem. _____

6. I clearly explain the actions I can take to solve the customer's problem. _____

7. I clearly explain what I cannot do to solve the customer's problem and the reasons why. _____

8. When I can't give the customer exactly what they want, I provide options and alternatives to help them solve their problem. _____

9. If I can't solve the customer's problem, I take responsibility for finding someone who can. _____

10. I keep customers informed as to the current status of the problem and follow-up when necessary. _____

11. I make suggestions as to how I feel our customer service can be improved. _____

12. When I cannot provide the customer with exactly what they want, I suggest options and alternatives. _____

13. I go the extra mile and take the extra step to help out my customer. _____

14. I use phrases such as "I understand," "I know how you feel," "I can see what you mean," and so on, to express empathy to the customer. _____

15. Regardless of who is at fault, I sincerely apologize to the customer when an error has been made. _____

16. To show that I am paying attention, I practice active listening by restating what the customer has said back to them. _____

17. I don't take the customer venting personally. _____

18. I avoid getting angry or argumentative when customers are voicing a complaint. _____

19. I view customer complaints as an opportunity rather than as a problem. _____

20. I view other departments and employees to whom I provide service as internal customers. _____

My total score is: _____

0–25 Points: Struggling

You're grasp on the basics may be a little rusty and in need of some repair. If you are a service newbie and still learning the ropes, practice the service skills highlighted in the questionnaire and use the information provided in this book and you'll be a pro in no time.

If you are an old hat, you may just be tired (or bored) and, in your weariness, found your way into some bad habits. Before you get to burnout, renew yourself by attending a customer service-training program, taking some time off, or asking your manager for the opportunity to work on a project you find exciting or interesting.

Lastly, if you read the evaluation questions and found yourself thinking "Why would I want to do that?" the field of customer service may not be for you. There are some people who, for whatever reason, just don't enjoy working with other people. If this sounds like you, seriously consider a career or job change.

26–40 Points: Solid

You seem to be aware of the basics, but don't always do them consistently. On some days, you provide stellar service, on others you just hope you get through the day without losing it. Feeling overwhelmed by too much to do, in too little time, may be the culprit. If this is the case, note the items in the questionnaire where you scored a "0" or "1" and make a point to practice these during the next month. Research shows that it takes 30 days to form a new habit, so regardless of the length of the interaction (two-minute phone call or 30-minute meeting) train yourself to switch into service mode.

41–60 Points: Stellar

Congratulations! You are a service star. You have a firm grasp on the basics and can handle more challenging customer situations. To grow beyond your current level of excellence try the following:

- Ask a close coworker to fill out this questionnaire on you. They may be able to highlight blind spots and areas for improvement.
- Retake the questionnaire but replace the word customer with coworker. Doing so will help you determine how good a job you are doing at providing internal service.

Find and Fix
E-mail Mistakes

The simplest way of checking your e-mail for mistakes is to read before you send and ask yourself, "How would I feel if I received this message?" E-mails, because they lack body language or tone of voice, are subject to misinterpretation. With e-mail 100 percent of the tone comes from the words you use and how you use them. Below are the eight most common e-mail mistakes along with their solutions:

1. **Unclear subject line**: The "title" of your e-mail should instantly convey what the message is about. Be sure to update the subject line as needed when you begin discussing a new topic. Negative headings such as "The Staff Meeting Sucked," are best left out.

2. **A poor greeting or no greeting at all:** Always begin your e-mails (even those addressing problems, crises, and concerns) with a friendly salutation. Despite the fact that it's electronic, e-mail is, at its core, a letter, and you would never think of sending one that did not start with "Dear John or Jane."

3. **Using abbreviations not commonly used or understood.** Take the extra time to spell out words or phrases instead of using uncommon abbreviations (such as technical jargon or in-house acronyms) the reader may not know.

16

4. **Unnecessary CCing:** Often, people courtesy copy (cc) others as a way of cyber-gossip or to vent their frustrations. No one is sitting at their desk wishing for more e-mails so don't waste the bandwidth of your fellow employees, only CC those people who are directly related to the situation or e-mail message.

5. **Sloppy grammar, spelling, and punctuation:** Sloppy e-mails, especially those with misspellings and poor grammar, lower your credibility rating. Everyone has hit the send button a little too soon and regretted it later. Taking a few seconds now to check your message upfront is insurance against embarrassment down the road.

6. **Using all capital letters:** Don't express strong feelings in uppercase. THEY CAN BE MISINTERPRETED!!! Using all caps to get across anger, frustration, and concern is the online equivalent of a "hissy fit." Instead consider picking up the phone to discuss difficult matters.

7. **No closing or sign off:** Just as important as a friendly greeting, a friendly closing is essential in your e-mail. You should always end your e-mail on a positive note—no matter what the content of the message.

8. **Difficult to read:** Disorganized messages that ramble on don't respect the reader's time and run the risk of losing their interest. Run-on sentences, repeated points, and absence of paragraph formatting make e-mails difficult to read.

Focus on Essence

At the heart of service excellence is the attitude that the customer is the most important part of your job. You can smile like the Cheshire cat and use all the right words, but if your underlying point of view is "This would be a great place to work if it wasn't for all those customers wanting to buy stuff," the message will come through loud and clear.

In order to understand how to create an authentic customer-friendly attitude, it's necessary to step back and look at what you do during the day. Do you attend meetings, write e-mails, answer questions, resolve problems? Take a minute to add a few things from your own work life to this list. For example, if we were to follow you around with a video camera from the moment you arrived at work until the moment you left, what tasks would you be doing? Please list a few below:

Attend Meetings   E-mail

Respond to Questions   Solve problems

_____   _____

_____   _____

_____   _____

The tasks that make up your day are the functions of your job. They are the routine, everyday way you get your job done and are often what you get measured on and rewarded for. Thinking that all the paperwork, data entry, and meetings you attend are the whole story is tempting. As you take a deeper look at these functions, you will see two common threads that run through 99.99 percent of them.

17

Thread 1: Communicating With Others

Regardless of what you do during the day, communication is at the heart of many work activities. Call a customer on the phone, that's verbal communication; send an e-mail, that's written communication. Walk into your mangers office and notice the scowl on his face—that's communication as well.

Thread 2: Establishing Relationships

The second common thread that runs through most of what you do during the day is creating relationships with other people. Not necessarily a deep, profound relationship, but rather making a connection with another person in order to accomplish something. That connection can be very brief and seemingly insignificant. For example, when you are a customer and you call a company up on the telephone, how long does it take you to get an impression of the person with whom you are speaking? If you are like most people, it usually takes just a few seconds. Aren't there some people who, when they say hello, you find yourself thinking, *"I'm not sure this person is going to be helpful."*

So, while doing the functions of your job well is important, they are only a means to an end. The real heart or essence of the job is communicating with people and establishing relationships. in the hurly, burly mad rush of day to day work, it's easy to forget this, focus on the functions, and begin to view the customer as an interruption of the job.

Think about a time when you were a customer and were treated as an interruption of the service provider's job. How did it feel? Have you ever been treated by a coworker as an interruption of their job?

In the end, the attitude you choose to focus on is one of the only things you have control over. Remembering that the customer is your job, and not an interruption of it, sets the foundation for service excellence in the largest Fortune 500 company or smallest mom-and-pop store.

Gather Feedback

The first step in improving service is to know—rather than assume—what your customers want and expect. The second step is know how well you are meeting those expectations. You can gather customer feedback through:

- Telephone interviews
- E-mail surveys
- Web surveys
- Face-to-face interviews
- Focus groups

In addition to discovering what's lurking in the hearts and minds of your customers, exploring how your staff feels is also important. Conducting staff surveys gives you a cultural X-ray into your overall customer focus.

Once you've gathered and analyzed the feedback, close the communication loop by getting back to the respondents with a summary of the results. Doing this tells them you heard what they said and encourages them to

Survey Strategies

In order to make your surveys effective, keep the following in mind:

- Keep all written questionnaires (including e-mail and Web) brief. If possible limit to 12 questions or less.
- Ensure confidentiality by not requiring customers or staff to put their name on the survey forms.
- Make it easy for people to fill out a survey by using a rating scale of 1 to 4, with space for comments. Avoid 1 to 5 because it tempts people to go with the middle ground (and pick 3).
- Get back to your customers and staff with an overview of the survey results and the actions you plan on taking based on their feedback.
- If you want more information on developing a survey (including samples) check out the authors' bestselling book *Customer Service For Dummies—Third Edition* (Wiley & Sons, 2006).

participate the next time you ask them to fill out a similar survey. For example:

One pharmaceutical company did an extensive customer survey of their mass-merchandising customers. After digesting the feedback, the company invited their customers to attend a meeting where they presented the survey results and conclusions. Almost all those invited attended. As a byproduct of conducting the survey and sharing the results (both good and bad) the company enjoyed a stronger partnership and enhanced image with their mega-retailer customers.

Thought-Starters

1. Do we regularly survey our customers to find out how satisfied they are with our service/products?
2. Do we have an effective process for evaluating the company's handling of complaints so that the results are translated into preventive measures?
3. Do we regularly survey our employees to find out how satisfied they are with their jobs, their managers, and the company?
4. Do we regularly meet with our employees to get their ideas on how our service and products can be improved?
5. Do we collect data on the aspects of our service that are statistically measurable, such as telephone waiting times, on-time delivery, and so on?

Get to Know the People Pleaser

People with this style are responsive and friendly, but not necessarily forceful or direct (think Katie Couric). They are good collaborators who thrive in a team environment. Telltale signs of a People Pleaser include:

- Friendly facial expressions and frequent eye contact.
- Non-aggressive, non-dramatic hand gestures.
- Slow speech with soft tones and moderate inflection.
- Supportive and encouraging language.
- Flexible about time.
- Believing that personal feelings are important when making decisions.
- Quiet in meetings.
- Inviting others to express opinions.
- Synthesizing idea of others who have spoken.
- A preference for one-on-one interactions or small groups versus large groups.

The strength of those with this style is their sensitivity to the feelings of others. They are generally good listeners whom coworkers and customers seek out for support. Because People Pleasers are skilled at cooperation and diplomacy, they are well-suited to the helping professions, such as nurses, therapists, customer service representatives, and teachers.

The downside is that they are reluctant to deal with conflict and disagreement and can have trouble asserting their ideas and opinions. Consequently, People Pleasers can be slow to make decisions and their frustrations with unresolved issues can turn into passive resentment.

Exercise:

To get more familiar with this style, think of someone you know who might have a People Pleaser style. Do they have a relatively low degree of assertiveness and a high degree of emotional expression?

What behaviors have you observed that indicate they have this style?

What do you admire about this person's style?
What do you have trouble with?

Go the Extra Mile

Treating your customers as the most important part of your job, fixing their problem and showering them with courtesy earns you a pat on the back for good service.

The difference between good and excellent service is the amount of initiative you take. *Initiative* is the ability or attitude required to begin something without being prompted. It's going the extra mile and taking the extra step for your customer—especially when things are on the right track already!

Regardless of the size of your company, initiative is easy to implement. All you need is the right attitude and an eye for opportunity. For example:

> *A contractor who understood that his industry was notorious for less-than-stellar service used initiative to insure his reputation for excellence. Before beginning a remodel job (and before punching the time clock), he sat down with customers to go over his step-by-step time plan for their project including major milestones, possible problem areas, and his contingency plans for dealing with them.*
>
> *By going the extra mile and educating his customers about the process (something his larger competitors failed to do), he separated himself from the pack.*

Customer Service In An Instant

Some companies employ a more extensive approach to implementing initiative by providing small tokens of appreciation. Customers take note of these unexpected extras and it pays off in increased loyalty—and referrals. For example:

A music company sent more than 1,000 holiday greeting cards to their customers, all signed by hand and including the individual names of each family member.

For larger corporations, a formalized, enterprise-wide initiative program often requires a considerable investment of time and money but can provide unexpected benefits for both customers and employees. For example:

An international hotel chain required employees to take personal responsibility for providing guests with any little extras that would make their stay first class. To this end, each staff member was allowed to spend up to $100 per guest, without permission and at his or her discretion, to satisfy the customer. The hotel chain was consistently rated among the top five in the world and staff turnover was lower than industry average.

Initiative on a Shoestring

Initiative doesn't have to cost an arm and a leg. The following ideas can build your reputation without breaking the bank.

- Give discount coupons.
- E-mail personalized messages with links to Web articles in which you know your customers would be interested.
- Offer free gift wrapping.
- When a loyal client needs something right away, overnight it and offer to pick up the charges.
- Send out pens, calculators, refrigerator magnets, and so on, that include your logo and contact information.
- Mail a hand-written greetings card on your clients' birthdays, offering a discount on their next purchase.
- Provide complimentary valet parking at busy times of the year.

Handle Complaints With Care

Research shows that for every complaint you receive, there are 25 more that you never hear. When a customer complains, they are giving you the opportunity to fix something they think is broken. Taking complaints seriously provides your company with valuable feedback and can stop a customer from switching to a competitor.

Dealing with customer complaints can be challenging. Here are five tips on how to listen and respond.

"YOU!" Doesn't Mean You

Regardless of the type of complainer you are dealing with, you are likely to get blamed for the problem. When the customer says "you" they mean your company, so stay focused on what he/she is saying and view the complaint as feedback rather than criticism. Resist the urge to interrupt or get defensive.

"Thank You" and "Sorry"

When the customer speaks up—rather than staying quiet—you can discover, fix, and improve the service that you offer. Sincerely thanking them for their feedback sets a positive tone that underscores your commitment to repairing any damage done.

An apology is also appropriate because the customer has not had his service expectations met. Saying you're sorry is not an admission of guilt. It lets the customer know that you understand the problem and the inconvenience it's caused.

Every Complaint Is Unique

Every customer's perception of a problem is unique, so don't jump ahead and assume that you already know what is going to be said. Listen to the complaint from beginning to end, taking notes and asking questions, even if you are so familiar with the problem you think it's not necessary.

Fix It, Don't Fight It

Once you have a good understanding of the complaint, reassure the customer that you are going to do everything within your power to fix it. Customers crave this reassurance and, as you discuss possible actions, they may have more to say. If so, don't argue or criticize, continue to listen and adjust your plan accordingly. Once you have agreed on a solution, use it—pronto!

Repair the System

The quality of your company's service is improved by fixing problems at the root cause. This means having a way to capture and resolve recurring complaints. For example: If the problem is inaccurate invoicing, the speedy dispatch of a corrected invoice might satisfy the customer, but it doesn't resolve the issue so that it doesn't happen again. A simple complaint-logging system is a good first-step in capturing complaints and then developing strategies for long-term improvement.

You can be a working part of that system by forwarding information on common complaints to your boss.

Hire Some Help

Be it classroom education, off-site meetings, videos, teleclasses, or Webinars, there are thousands of consulting firms, coaches, and training companies offering customer-service education. To insure that you get the best fit for your company, consider the following criteria in selecting your training vendor.

- **Expertise:** Does this firm specialize in customer-service training and consulting, or is it just one of the myriad of programs it offers? What is their background in this area and with whom have they worked? Ask for references you can call.

- **Delivery:** Who exactly will deliver the training programs, and what is their expertise and experience in this area? Many companies send one person to pitch its products, but another person to do the delivery.

- **Proposal:** Is the company willing to write a detailed proposal including course descriptions, timelines, and fees—at no charge? Does its proposal reflect important aspects of the project discussed?

- **Follow-Up:** What does the company offer in the way of follow-up? Does it have online support programs for post-course training? Are representatives available (for a fee, of course) to conduct one-on-one coaching as needed?

- **Customization:** What specific steps does this company take to customiz its programs to your needs and corporate culture? Does it use generic examples or ones specific to your industry and company?

Does it only offer limited training modules or can they create new ones as needed?

- **Style:** How does the company describe its training style? What combination of lecture, exercises, written work, and role-playing is involved in its programs? How well does the style of the company seem to fit with the culture of yours?

Improve Your Listening Habits

Listening is a complex process that involves paying attention on many different levels. Not only to the words on the surface, but to the feelings (yours and the customers) underneath. Don't let bad listening habits hinder your customer service.

Listen for the Message Underneath

Not everyone has the oratory skills of an Abraham Lincoln. Accents, regional dialects, ums, uhs, and mispronounced words may not be a delight to your ears, but don't let them keep you from hearing what's really being said. Instead, listen for what your clients are saying rather than how they are saying it.

When people are upset, they don't always communicate clearly and calmly, so, if you need to ask your customer to slow down or repeat what they just said, do it with pleasant patience—not irritation. For example: "I'm sorry, I didn't catch that, could you repeat it please," works better than, "I don't understand what you are saying."

Filter for Feelings and Facts

It's tempting to try to filter out the feelings your customer is expressing (especially the negative ones such as anger, fear, and frustration) and just focus on the facts of their situation. The problem with this is that, for many customers, the recognition of their feelings is part and parcel of how they experience good service. Pay attention to what your customer's tone of voice and body language tells you about how he or she is feeling. While you don't need to dwell on your customer's emotional state, saying something such as, "I can see that this is really scary for you," shows empathy (see way 39) and validates how your customer is feeling.

Take Note

You may have graduated cum laude from that weekend "Master Your Memory" course, but to rely on your brains power of recall to remember the specific details of a customer conversation is asking for trouble down the road. While were not suggesting you write a thesis on your customers problem, it is always a good idea to jot down the important details of a conversation, such as dates, times, amounts, account numbers, and so on.

Interrupting

This is the fifth customer in a row to tell you that your voicemail isn't working. As they go on, giving you details you already know, you think to yourself, "Why waste time? I'll just stop them and skip ahead to the bottom line." Right?

Wrong. Interrupting by finishing the customer's thought or cutting them off mid sentence may save time but costs customer confidence.

Inspire a Learning Environment

Malcolm Knowles, a pioneering figure in adult education, is often referred to as "the Father of Adult Learning" and was a proponent of adult educators functioning as facilitators. In his book *Modern Practice* he wrote "At its best, an adult learning experience should be a process of self-directed inquiry, with the resources of the teacher, fellow students, and materials being available to the learner, but not imposed on him."

Too often, managers try to improve their staff's service skills with a single magic bullet consisting of one day of training, single session mentoring, or the old- fashioned "sink or swim." Modern Managers can borrow a page from Knowles's book by creating learning environments that involve a multitude of methods.

In the following example, Carrie, the supervisor of the production department, wants to teach Carl, one of his senior staff members, to run the Friday Production meetings. Carrie can use a combination of the methods listed below to achieve this objective.

Learning by Experience

Characterized by on the job practice, the student learns by trial and error. Successes are celebrated and failures evaluated.

Activity: Carrie and Carl co-run the production meeting together and debrief afterward.

Observing Role Models

Many people learn by observing the actions and behaviors of others around them who are experts in the skills they want to improve.

Activity: Carrie leads the meeting and Carl observes—taking notes and asking questions afterward.

Passive Instruction

This type of learning takes place when the individual receives instruction by reading, listening, or viewing a multimedia program, usually on their own.

Activity: Carrie gives Carl a book and an online training program on how to conduct meetings.

Reflection and Discussion (Coaching)

Much can be learned from talking with others about your successes and failures.

Often this method of learning takes place in a relaxed and informal environment and involves one-on-one conversation, usually between the manager and staff.

Activity: Carrie observes Carl leading a production meeting and then, afterward, praises him for what he did well and offers constructive suggestions on how he could improve next time.

Formal Training

Extremely valuable as a baseline for learning, training is most powerful when conducted in tangent with other independent learning methods. Any training worth it's salt provides a combination of role-playing, exercises, discussion, and technology.

Activity: Carrie and Carl attend a class offered by the companies Human Resources Department on meeting management.

Integrate Voicemail Excellence

To advocates, voicemail is a saving grace that increases productivity and reduces interruptions. To adversaries, it's a customer-service killer that discourages personal communication and can lead to lag times. Regardless, it's here to stay. One study conducted by AT&T showed that three out of four calls at work are not completed on the first try. To make the most of voicemail, put these best practices in place.

Answer Your Phone—At Least Some of the Time

Although it's not always possible or practical to answer your own phone, good customer care requires that you personally pick up your calls at least several times during the day. When you do, you send a positive message of availability.

Keep Your Greeting Updated

If you are going to be away from the office for a prolonged period of time, always make sure your greeting includes the date you will return. Remember to update your message once you are back.

Respond to Messages Within 24 Hours

Depending on the nature and urgency of the call, if your callers don't receive responses within a reasonable period of time (usually

24 hours), they will begin to assume that voicemail is an ineffective way of communicating with you.

Encourage People to E-mail You Details

In their effort to leave a detailed message that covers all the important points, many people leave long-winded, rambling messages. Prevent this by encouraging people to e-mail you with any details they think you might find helpful.

Provide Options

People will leave clearer and more detailed messages if they have a chance to review what they've said before they send. If possible, allow the caller to press a number that permits them to review their message before committing it to recording. Also, always give callers the option of pressing 0 for the operator, or another extension that gets them out of the voicemail labyrinth and connected to a real person.

Keep Your Greeting Relatively Short and to the Point

"Hi, this is Karen. I'm not here right now. I'm on a yak photography safari. If you leave a short message, the day and time you called, a good time to reach you, and your phone number (even if you think I have it), I will get back to you at my earliest convenience, when I return from Siberia on Tuesday, June 15th. I won't be picking up e-mails, so if you need assistance please contact my assistant, Jean, at ext. 515 with any questions or concerns, or e-mail her at jean@scgtraining.com. In the future, you can skip this message by pressing the pound sign. Thank you for calling and have a nice day."

This is the long-winded approach and reads like *War and Peace*. At the opposite extreme, some messages are so short, they seem curt:

"Hi, this is Karen. Leave a message."

For a happy medium, record a greeting that provides the essential information concisely:

"Hi, this is Karen. I'm out of the office until June 15th. Please leave me a short message and your number. I will get back to you at my earliest convenience. If this is urgent please contact Jean at ext. 515."

26

Keep the Service Message Alive

One of the challenges facing managers is how to maintain a high level of customer satisfaction day in, day out. Training is an effective way to teach customer-service skills, but monthly "service improvement" meetings between managers and staff are also needed to keep the message alive.

These meetings can focus on any topic related to service. Some ideas include:

- Debrief and learn from both good and bad service experiences.
- Work together to solve a specific service problem.
- Role-play difficult customer situations.
- Brainstorm new solutions to old problems.

Here are six tips to make your monthly service meetings more interesting, participative, and productive.

1. **Create an agenda:** Pave the way for a successful meeting by creating an agenda and sending it out ahead of time. The agenda should include: the purpose of the meeting, the intended results, questions you want the group to consider ahead of time, timeline, date, and location.

2. **Keep the meeting brief:** Meetings that last between 15 and 30 minutes are perfect. Short meetings stop people from getting bored, help keep things moving, allow for easier scheduling, and require you to focus on one topic at time, instead of bombarding the group with a mondo-agenda!

3. **Make the meeting fun:** Nobody looks forward to a snooze-fest! A lively meeting keeps people awake and interested in what is being presented. Try grabbing your group's attention by telling a personal story or giving a specific example that relates to the topic of the meeting. For example, tell a story of a recent time when you were a customer and received terrible service. Everyone seems to love a good horror story!

4. **Get the group talking:** A dialogue is a lot more enjoyable than a monologue. For example: Do a flip-flop and, after sharing your personal service nightmare, ask the group to share their personal examples. People listen better once they are engaged in a two-way conversation. Remember, talk *to* people, not *at* them.

5. **Write it down, sum it up:** Using a flipchart or notepaper jot down some of the key points highlighted in the group meeting. Review the list at the end of the session and make sure everyone has something from the list they can walk away with and use back on the job.

6. **Keep the meeting on track:** If your group hits a hot button and the meeting devolves into a feeding frenzy of negative opinions and complaining, be prepared to step in and gently guide the group back on track.

Don't try to sweep the group's frustration under the carpet. Instead, acknowledge it and ask the group to refocus their efforts on the issue at hand.

Know Your Stress Response

How many times have you brought your car to a screeching halt because you thought you were about to squash a squirrel? You feel a jolt of adrenaline, your heart beats faster, and your hands get clammy...only to discover that the "endangered roadway rodent" was only a paper bag!

Whenever you sense danger, the primitive hypothalamus gland, located at the base of your skull, releases chemicals into the bloodstream that give you the strength and power to react. Your body's response to stress hasn't evolved much since cave-man days. While you no longer face the daily danger of being eaten alive by a saber-toothed tiger, your brain and body still run on two fundamental survival strategies—fight or flee.

For example, if a customer is being difficult, you might start thinking, "I just want to walk away" (flee) or " I should just tell this guy to calm down, be quiet, and listen up" (fight). Given that neither of these "survival" tactics is a smart option, your body doesn't know what to do with the "get-up-and-go" chemicals that have now been set loose in your bloodstream.

The problem is that the hypothalamus gland reacts to input that is both real—and imagined. The paper bag in the road wasn't an animal, but, as long as your brain thought it was, you reacted accordingly. Think about the last time you watched a scary movie. You had all the physical sensations associated with fear (increased heart rate, sweaty palms, clenched jaw) even though you knew that the big, bad monster up on the screen was made of film, not flesh.

One last example: Imagine it is Friday afternoon, and you receive a message from your boss that he wants to see you right away. By the time you get the message, he has left on a wild-man wilderness trek and won't be back until Monday. During the weekend you wonder what you did wrong and worry, as you run countless scenarios through your mind.

Monday morning, you arrive early and seek your boss first thing, so you can put yourself out of your misery. Imagine your relief when your boss offers you a hearty handshake and congratulations on what a bang-up job you did on that quarterly report!

The point is that you can experience very real stress, even if the cause is your imagination run amok or negative self-talk. Your hypothalamus gland doesn't care. Its job is to automatically react to whatever input it receives.

Although there will always be "real" stresses at work, you can help reduce your overall stress level by not adding your negative interpretations or negative filters to the given circumstances.

Learn the Art of Complaining

Being a courteous complainer when you're the consumer builds character and helps you identify with your customers' plights. As with anything, practice makes perfect. The next time you find yourself in a problematic position, speak up and help make the world safer for service. To master the art of competent complaining:

Write Down the Details

Nothing makes your complaint sing like well-documented details. Names, dates, and times all say to the company, "I have paid attention to the specifics of my situation and so should you." Remember, you make it easy for the customer-service representative to discount your creditability when you can't tell them who did what to whom, where, and when.

The flip side: If your customer is not writing down the important details you're discussing, gently suggest that they do so.

Be a Polite, Squeaky Wheel

Most service representatives carry the scars of battles fought with angry customers. Clearly asking for what you want with courtesy, it's often enough to melt even the hardest of hearts. While there's no need to be overly accommodating, polite will get you farther faster. Be clear, concise, and firm about what you want and use the resources of the service person to help you get it. Try asking:

What do you recommend I do?

How do you suggest I handle this?

Can you tell me what a good next step is?

What would you do in my situation?

The flip side: Upset customers don't usually present their problems in a nice, neat package with a bow around the box and a thank-you card attached. More often they grumble, grouse, and ramble. You can move the problem-solving process along and reduce the tension of the situation by prompting your customer to identify and focus on the outcomes they want. Let them know that you will do your best, within your power, to help them get it.

Move Up the Ladder

When you hit the wall of incompetence, inexperience, or inability, it's time to move your complaint up the ladder. The easiest route is to enlist the aid of the service person. Avoid putting them on the defensive by saying "Clearly, you are not the right person to help me with this, let me talk to your supervisor!" A better approach is to garner their support by saying, "I appreciate everything you have done to help me, but at this point I think it might save us both some time if I spoke with a manger or supervisor. Who would you recommend I talk to, and can you tell me where to reach them?"

If all else fails, Google the company, locate the corporate headquarters, call the president or vice president's office, and speak to his or her secretary. It's this person's job to prevent people like you from spending the CEO's time, and they will more than likely handle the situation themselves—getting you the results you desire.

The flip side: There is a big difference between referring a customer up a rung in order to get them off your back (not that you would ever do that) and realizing that it's in their best interest to take their complaint to the next level. If you do need to move your customer upward and onward, give them all the information they need (name, phone, e-mail) for the person who you think will best be able to resolve their problem.

Locate Your Stress Level

A large-scale survey conducted by University College, London, found that chronically stressed workers had a 68-percent higher risk of developing heart disease than moderately stressed ones.

Customer Service In An Instant

Your stress level is affected by a variety of factors: difficult customers and coworkers, the physical work environment, how organized you are, your level of job satisfaction, how well you get along with your boss, and so on. To get a read on your current level of work stress, answer yes or no to the following questions:

1. Do continual interruptions distract you from your work?

    o Yes   o No

2. Is it usual for you to work through lunch?

    o Yes   o No

3. Do you drink more than three cups of coffee a day?

    o Yes   o No

4. Do you often run over deadlines on important projects?

    o Yes   o No

5. Do you feel that your boss doesn't listen to the suggestions you make?

    o Yes   o No

6. Do you often work more than five consecutive days a week?

    o Yes   o No

7. Do you regularly put in extra time during weekend or evenings?

       o Yes   o No

8. Do you easily get frustrated or angry when working with upset customers?

       o Yes   o No

9. Does your job involve meeting constant deadlines?

       o Yes   o No

10. Do you feel trapped in your job?

       o Yes   o No

11. Is your work area really loud?

       o Yes   o No

12. Do you regularly feel overwhelmed at work by multitasking too many responsibilities?

       o Yes   o No

13. Is it difficult or impossible to delegate work when you need to?

       o Yes   o No

14. Do you easily get impatient with customers and coworkers?

       o Yes   o No

15. Do you regularly run late for important activities or appointments?

    o Yes   o No

16. Is it hard for you to have a conversation with your boss?

    o Yes   o No

17. Are you weighed down by the responsibility of your job?

    o Yes   o No

18. Do you dread the thought of going to your job?

    o Yes   o No

19. Do you regularly get stress headaches, tight neck, and so on?

    o Yes   o No

20. Do you feel that you spend too much time at work?

    o Yes   o No

To score the test, assign one point for each yes answer you checked.

0–5 Points: Green Zone

Your current level of stress is low, and you probably make a point of practicing stress management techniques. Keep up the great work.

6–12 Points: Yellow Zone

Your current level of stress is about average, but may still be higher than you would like. To reduce it, go to your local bookstore or library and check out some books on stress management or take a one-day class in stress-reducing techniques.

13–20 Points: Red Zone

Your current level of stress is high and may be affecting your health. Don't try and tough it out, instead go over the items to which you checked yes and determine some initial changes you could make. For example: take scheduled breaks from work for eating and relaxing, take up a relaxation practice such as yoga or meditation, or make a point to discuss what is making you feel stressed with a close colleague or friend.

Five Minutes to Less Stress

Watch the sunset.
Sing along with the radio.
Pet a dog.
Listen to music.
Take a nap.
Dance up a storm.
Go for a walk.
Have a cup of tea.
Ask for help.
Take a break.
Stand up and stretch.
Write your feelings in a journal.
Meditate.

See a movie.
Play with a child.
Say no.
Read a book.
Light a candle.
Laugh out loud.
Talk to a friend.
Take a bath.
Breath deeply.
Ask for what you need.
Walk a labyrinth.
Give a compliment.
Clean our your desk.

Make Your Service Tangible

Translating general service qualities into specific service standards is a powerful way of shaping the image that your customers have of you and your company. General service qualities describe the basic ways you treat your customers. For example:

- Greet customers with a friendly attitude.
- Be prompt in responding to customers' requests.
- Show understanding when listening to customer problems.
- Be responsive to customer needs.

While these are all worthy goals, they mean different things to different people. Service standards go one step further by turning general service qualities into specific, measurable actions. Here is a **three-step process** for developing your own service standards:

1. Map Out Your Service Sequence

The service sequence of your business is like the chapters of a book. They subdivide your customers overall experience into bite size pieces. For example, the basic service sequence in a restaurant includes:

- Check in with the host/hostess.
- Be seated.
- Order.

- Eat.
- Pay the check.

Exercise:

Thinking about your business from the customer's point of view, what would the separate pieces in the sequence be?

---

2. Define Key Actions

Just as every chapter of a book is made up of paragraphs, so each step along the way in a service sequence is made up of key actions. For example, the key actions for checking in with the host/hostess in a restaurant include:

- Customer approaches the host/hostess.
- Host/hostess asks for the customer's name and checks the reservations list.
- Host/hostess provides wait time information.

Exercise:

Now that you've broken your business up into its various chapters, choose one area that needs improvement and define, in chronological order, the actions that make up that particular customer encounter:

---

3. Add Experience-enhancers

In the previous restaurant example, no value has been added to the basic actions. It is simply an accurate, step-by-step description that reflects how every restaurant in the world seats a customer. Excellent customer care requires experience-enhancers.

For example, the first step in the sequence, "Customer approaches the host/hostess," is critical, because it creates a first impression. In order to add experience-enhancers, standards must be created:

- Smile at the customer as he or she approaches, make direct eye contact, and say "Good morning," "Good afternoon," or "Good evening." This standard conveys friendliness.

- Use the customer's name as soon as you know it. This standard conveys recognition and attentiveness.

- If the wait time is longer than five minutes, ask the customer if they would like to wait at the bar and have a drink. This standard shows initiative.

These sound simple, don't they? Well, they are, but never underestimate the power of simple, consistent standards and how they can make your business a service star in your customer's mind.

Exercise:

Rewrite the actions you defined to include specific, measurable service standards that serve to enhance the customer's experience.

_____

_____

_____

Moments of Truth

Every time a customer comes in contact with your company, it's a moment of truth, because it leaves them with either a positive memorable or a negative memorable impression. Not all moments of truth are created equal. Some are more critical to your customer's overall experience than others. For example, in a hotel, the speed and efficiency of the check-in process sets things off on the right foot—or not. In a technical support department, the ability to easily reach a real, live human being defines the customer's experience. By thinking about the key moments of truth in your business, you can discover critical areas on which to focus.

Manage Abusive Customers

Abusive customers are not your plain, old, garden-variety upset customers. They are people who have crossed the line and stormed into the territory of unacceptable behavior such as: personal insults, swearing and cursing, screaming and yelling, making threats, and saying unflattering things about your mother. While company policies may vary (check with yours) on the specific strategies for managing abusive customers, keep in mind the following do's and don'ts.

Offer to Help

Despite the customer's ranting, let them know, sincerely and clearly, that you really are trying to help.

Do say:

"I want to solve your problem, but I am having a hard time with this conversation, because of your cursing/shouting/threats, and so on.

Don't say:

"Your rude behavior will not help solve this problem. You need to calm down."

Send Them to a Supervisor

If, after several warnings, the customer continues his offensive behavior, it may be time to move him up to a supervisor.

Do say:

"I am sorry but I can't seem to help you. I am going to have you speak with my supervisor."

Don't say:

"I am not going to put up with you any longer. You're going to have to talk to my supervisor."

End the Interaction

If there isn't a supervisor available to take over, the next step is to politely end the conversation.

Do say:

"I want you to be satisfied with our service, but I'm unable to help, so I suggest you come/call back later."

Don't say:

"I am ending this conversation/call. I suggest you pull yourself together before you come/call back."

Bouncing Back After a Tough Conversation

Abusive customers can knock the wind out of you and ruin your whole day. Here are some quick ways to get yourself back on track.

Walk a While

A short walk provides a brief and healthy change of scenery that can shift your frame of mind. Even short periods of exercise (five to ten minutes) help you let go of pent up emotions so that you can return to work feeling refreshed.

Use Your Imagination

Find a private place where you can sit quietly for two minutes. Close your eyes and breathe slowly. As you breathe in, imagine a feeling of peacefulness. Let that feeling spread through your body.

Then, breathe out and imagine exhaling all the stress and unpleasant feelings. Do this several times until you feel calmer.

Grab More Oxygen

If you cannot leave your workstation or it's inconvenient to close your eyes, you can do a few breathing exercises right at your desk. Slowly inhale in through your nose while mentally counting to four. As you inhale let your stomach naturally expand outward, this helps your shoulders and neck to relax. Exhale through your mouth while counting to six.

Relax Your Muscles

Start by tensing the muscles in your face (yes, this looks strange, so skip this part of your body if you are in a meeting) and hold for six seconds. Next, exhale and relax your face completely. Feel the tension drain away. Use the same tense and release pattern for your neck, shoulders, chest, abdomen, legs, and feet.

Master Body Language Basics

Do you believe your eyes can listen? They can. In his book, *Silent Messages*, Albert Mehrabian reports that 55 percent of what you learn from others comes from their body language, 33 percent comes from tone of voice, and only 7 percent comes from the words spoken.

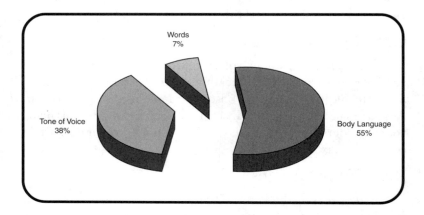

Remember how clearly you heard the hand gestures of the motorist you accidentally cut off this morning on your way to work? Even when the mouth is silent, the body speaks volumes. Here are some classic examples:

- The waitress at your favorite breakfast haunt rolls her eyes when you ask for your eggs a-little-on-the-soft-side-of-hard-but-not-too-runny.

- Your dry cleaner's face scrunches up into a tight ball as you enthusiastically drop off the 2,000 wire hangers for recycling.

- Your car mechanic dives under the hood of your car and doesn't come up for air as you explain where the smoke and sparks where coming from.

Learn to project your own body language in a way that says, "I want to help you," instead of "Drop dead!" It's one of the least-expensive and most-useful customer-service skills you have.

Here are the key parts of body language and what they convey:

Body Language	Negative	Positive
Eye Contact	Lack of eye contact tells your customers you don't care and you're not paying attention. Be careful not to stare; it's zombie-like and rude.	Look at your customers to let them know that you are interested and concerned.
Facial Expression	Rolling your eyes, furrowing your brow, sneering, looking dismayed, pained, or confused are all expressions that send a negative message.	A smile or a relaxed facial expression is the best way to go. If the customer has a problem and is upset, then a concerned look works better than a big grin!
Body Posture	Turning away from your customers gives the impression that you're ignoring them or not interested.	If you want to win big points, learn to lean forward, face the customer, or turn in their direction—especially when you are busy doing something else.
Nodding	Nodding can be overdone or underdone. If you nod non-stop, you communicate impatience. If you *never* nod you convey lack of attention.	Nod from time to time to let customers know that you are listening and concerned. This is especially useful when a customer is upset and has a lot to say.
Physical Distance	Customers don't like it when their "personal space" is encroached upon. Closer than three feet (think elevator), makes customers feel uncomfortable.	Maintain an arms length between you and your customers. If you notice them moving further and further back, then stop moving towards them!

Navigate a Heated Conversation

Navigating your way through a heated conversation can be like crossing a minefield—one wrong step and all hell breaks loose. The following road map weaves together several stand-alone techniques into a process that will guide you through the twists and turns to arrive at a successful conclusion.

Let 'Em Vent

Customers want their problem fixed, but they also want to vent their feelings. The pressure they feel to let off steam is often so strong that your safest route is to stay quiet and give them lots of room to decompress. You can let them know you are interested and listening by occasionally saying "uh-huh." If you are in a face-to-face interaction be sure to maintain eye contact and nod from time to time as well. Stay on course by resisting the itch to interrupt—*especially* if they light a spark in you by saying:

- You are the worst person I have ever dealt with in this company.
- They didn't train you very well.
- Let me talk to someone who is more competent.
- Since when did they start hiring idiots?

Switch Filters

Irate customers can say and do things that might convince you they are the lowest form of human life. Your disapproving opinion becomes a Negative Filter that fans the flames and moves you further away from a happy ending. Stay focused on the customer's underlying needs by switching filters and silently asking yourself: "What does this person need and how can I provide it to the best of my ability?"

Show Empathy

After your customer has let off steam and you have switched any Negative filters to Service Filters, it is safe to begin speaking. Start by showing empathy for the customer's situation. Put yourself in their shoes; let them know you understand what they are saying and why they are upset. Empathy absorbs emotion and leads to dialogue.

Start Solving

Having acknowledged the customer's feelings, it is now time to begin solving their problem. Start by asking clarifying questions and avoiding the temptation to form conclusions before you have heard the whole story. Assuming that you already know the answer diminishes your listening power and prevents you from hearing important details.

Mutually Agree

Now that you know the facts, present the customer with a solution for consideration. If there are different solution options, present the pros and cons of each,7 so the customer can make an informed choice. For example, in a conversation about a customer's computer repair, the service representative might present the following three options:

1. Ship the computer back to our company. *Pros:* The repair will be factory authorized. *Cons:* You will have to box it up for shipping and it will take three weeks to fix.

2. Take the computer to your local dealer. *Pros:* The repair will be factory authorized and you can talk with them, in person, about the repair. *Cons:* The repair

time will depend on how busy they are. Your nearest dealership is 20 miles away.

3. Order the part and fix it yourself. *Pros:* This is less expensive and faster than the other two options. *Cons:* This is not a factory authorized repair so, if you replace the part incorrectly and something goes wrong, the factory will not be able to fix it for you.

Follow Up

Whenever possible, service stars follow-up with their customers to ensure that the solution worked satisfactorily. If it did, then the follow-up acts as a courtesy call. If it didn't, alternative solutions are needed. In either case, the message to the customer is: We care, and the buck stops here.

Open to Feedback

Named after its inventors, Joseph Luft and Harry Ingham, the Johari Window is a well-respected model that helps people improve their interpersonal communication. A four paned "window," divides personal awareness into quadrants: open, hidden, blind, and unknown.

The "open" quadrant represents things that you—and other people—know about you. For example, you know that, under pressure, you become a bit sulky. From years of observation, your co-workers, no doubt, know this as well.

The "hidden" quadrant represents things that you know about yourself—but others don't. For example, when things get really tough at work, you sneak out for a quick chocolate fix.

The "unknown" quadrant represent things that you don't see about yourself—neither do those around you. For example, you get irate when your boss leaves messages on your home voicemail. You don't understand why such a simple thing feels so significant.

The "blind" quadrant represents things that others know about you—but of which you are unaware. For example, when you feel nervous in a meeting, you unknowingly tap your foot, irritating everyone around you.

It is in this last quadrant where getting feedback from your bosses, peers and even customers can help reveal your blind spots and open a window to growth. But feedback, especially if it is about something you could have done better, can be hard to hear. To make it easier try the following:

- Ask for specific examples of the behavior the person is talking about. It's hard to make a change if you don't know what to do.

- Ask for clarification. If you don't fully understand what the other person is saying, ask a combination of open- and close-ended questions to get a clearer picture of their criticism.

- Relax your body. It's easy to tense up when being told something you may not like hearing. Try and consciously use your breath to remain relaxed.

- Limit defensiveness. While you may want to explain (without excuses) what happened, there is no need to justify or defend your behavior to the other person.

- Long, convoluted explanations invite long, convoluted discussions. As much as you are able, listen to what the other person has to say, say what you need to say, and leave the rest.

- Reflect back. Let the person know that you have heard what they said, whether you agree with them or not, by paraphrasing their feedback. At this point, you may even agree with some (if not all) of their criticism. If you do, don't be afraid to say so.

- Thank the person for their feedback. Even if the other person is not an expert at delivering constructive criticism (and the message was conveyed with the best of intentions), thank them for their feedback. Letting the other person know you appreciate their taking the time, energy, and courage to speak to you has deepened your trust in each other.

Pace Your Way to Better Rapport

Pacing is a vital skill for connecting with your customers quickly and creating rapport. The stronger that connection, the more willing they are to hear what you have to say—especially if they are upset. The challenge then is to understand each person's unique view of the world. For example, when you see the following word, what comes to mind?

RED

A fire truck, danger, traffic lights, blood, roses, apples, a stop sign, or hundreds of other things, may have popped into your mind. Everyone sees the same word but it conjures up different images. If your customer sees RED and thinks roses, but you think fire engines, how do you get on the same page? Pacing helps you bridge this gap, even if you don't know anything about the other person. Here's how it works.

Imagine two strangers sitting next to each other on a plane. They have two "maps" of how they see the world.

The conversation usually starts with, "Where are you going?" or "Where are you from?" or "Are you really going to eat that?" These two passengers are asking these questions to create rapport by discovering places where their understanding of the world, or their "maps," overlap. When you find similarities with others, you feel more at ease and more connected.

Customer's World   Serivice Provider's World

Overlap is where rapport takes place

To pace, approximately and respectfully, match the other person's body language and tone of voice. By doing this you are silently saying, "I am like you" and this creates comfort and trust.

Example 1

You are meeting with a coworker about a scheduling issue. She tells you she is having a problem finding a replacement to cover her weekend shift. As she talks, you notice she is speaking quickly and sitting forward in her chair. Her arms are by her side, and they move very little during the conversation.

You pace her by moving forward in your chair and sitting up (instead of sitting back, which is more normal for you). You usually use big arm gestures but in this case pacing requires that you keep your gestures to a minimum. Also, instead of speaking at your normal mellow pace, you speed up to match your co-worker.

Example 2

You are having a phone conversation with a customer who is confused about your product. He is speaking slowly and deliberately and using non-technical terms.

You pace him by slowing down your normally fast rate of speech. Because you detect confusion his voice, you speak clearly and deliberately, using as few technical terms as possible.

Humans are creatures of habit who like what is familiar. Ultimately, pacing is about presenting yourself to the other person in a way that is believable and true—in their perception.

Pace First, Lead Last

Pacing creates rapport because you follow the other person's lead. Leading, on the other hand, shifts this dynamic, and you become the person moving the conversation forward. Whenever you present an idea, make a suggestion, or offer a solution, you are leading the conversation.

When you are pacing, natural lulls in the conversation offer an opportunity to try leading. If the timing is right, your customer will naturally begin to pace you. If your timing is off, they will continue to lead. Your job at that point is to go back to pacing them—again. Remember effective leading mostly happens after a period of pacing. The pattern goes something like this:

Pace, pace, pace, lead.
Pace, pace, lead, lead.
Lead, lead, lead,—pace!

Pay Attention, Really

Just because you smile, politely nod, and say uh huh, does not mean that you are really listening. Customers are quick to catch on when you are *faking* attention. Often you don't notice the attention grabbers around you; they fade into the background because you have learned to put up with them. The trick is to become aware of what is stealing your attention and fix it, if you can. The most common hurdles to paying attention include:

- **Environment:** When the air conditioning vent above your head makes your workspace below feel like Antarctica, it can be hard to focus. Your physical space, including temperature, chair comfort, and keyboard placement (too low or too high) all have an impact. Besides finding out who controls the temperature in your building and becoming their new best friend, go ergonomic and get a chair, keyboard, and mouse that are designed to support your body.

- **Cluttered Work Area:** Believe it or not, the visual distraction of a messy desktop can steal away attention. While your work area does not need to look like a Fortune Magazine layout of an organized office, chaos should be kept to minimum by keeping paperwork, files, and piles relatively neat and organized.

- **Noise:** Ringing telephones, honking horns, and the sound of coworkers voices coming from the next cubical. Even low-level noise can make it difficult to fully concentrate on the person to whom you're talking.

Reducing some noise may be out of your control, but small actions, such as shutting a window, getting a pair of noise canceling headphones or asking you co-worker to turn down the volume, can help.

- **The Other Person:** Sometimes the people you are trying to focus on become the distraction themselves. Poor hygiene, bad grooming, nervous habits, and odd physical mannerisms can pull you out of listening mode and into judging mode. That judging mode can lead to Negative Filters and a downward spiral of your interaction with the other person.

- **E-mail and the Internet:** If you're talking on the phone and simultaneously surfing the net or clicking away on a keyboard, the other person can feel and hear it! The split second lag time in your response is noticeable. Take a Zen approach and do one thing at a time.

- **Stress:** Some of the distractions you experience are internal and include preoccupation with personal problems, anxiety about something that is going on at work, boredom with your job, and so on. You can *choose* to dwell on these focus-stealers and make them significant, or you can retune your focus to the needs of the person in front of you. In order to get to this point, you may need to take a few actions including:
  - Speak with a trusted coworker or friend about what is bothering you.
  - Actively seek support from your human resources department.
  - Contact your employee-assistance program.

Play With the Passionate Persuader

People with this style have a lively and outgoing nature, which often motivates and creates excitement in others (think Oprah). They are enthusiastic, friendly, and prefer working with other people, rather than alone. Tell tale signs of a Passionate Persuader include:

- Rapid hand movements and big arm gestures.
- Quick speech with lots of animation and inflection.
- Wide range of facial expressions.
- Flowing, dramatic language.
- Strong and passionate expression of opinions.
- Quick decision-making, often based on intuition.
- Deep involvement in whatever project is in front of them.
- Telling stories and jokes.
- Energy in abundance.
- Initiating projects and goals.

The strength of those with this style lies in their ability to build alliances and relationships to accomplish their goals. Because they work at a fast pace and thrive in the spotlight, Passionate Persuaders are well suited to high profile positions that require them to make public presentations. For this reason, they often gravitate towards professions such as training, performing, and selling.

The downside is that, when upset or anxious, Passionate Persuaders communicate their feelings with intensity. If they feel criticized, they can be overly harsh in their response. People with a less-assertive working style may find them overwhelming to deal with. Once a Passionate Persuader wraps their mind around an idea, they are quick to make it happen and can overlook important details and overrun others' opinions.

Exercise:

To get more familiar with this style, think of someone you know who might have a Passionate Persuader style and answer the questions that follow. Do they have a relatively high degree of assertiveness and a relatively high degree emotional expression?

What behaviors have you observed that indicate they have this style?

What do you admire about this person's style?

What do you have trouble with?

Practice the Art of the Compliment

There is nothing more motivating for your staff, coworkers, or customers as receiving the gift of a good compliment.

Delivered face to face, by phone, letter, or e-mail, a compliment that goes beyond the generic good job—and gives specific details—is a service skill worth mastering. To practice the art of the compliment keep in mind:

Specifics Win the Day

Instead of saying "well done," take the time to notice what, in particular, was noteworthy. Adding specifics always strengthens a compliment. For example: "You did a great job handling that customer. I really liked the way you let her talk out her problem, before offering solutions." Some good compliment starters include:

- Congratulations on...
- You did a wonderful job with...
- I have great admiration for...
- I am grateful for...
- I really admire your...
- I am impressed with...
- I really appreciate your...

It's All About
Character and Qualities

Perhaps the most memorable compliment is the one that recognizes who the other person is, rather than what they do. To make a specific complement even more meaningful, include recognition of the other person's character. For example: " I really appreciate your waiting. You have been very *patient* and *understanding* through this whole matter." Some good character compliments include:

- You have a way with words.
- You are a good leader.
- It's fun having you on the team.
- You live up to your reputation.
- It's obvious that you know what you are doing.
- You are a good listener.
- You are funny.

Consider the following complement with no bells and whistles attached.

"Bob—great job at the meeting this morning."

Nice enough, but if you take it one step further and add all the elements of an artful compliment, you end up with something far more impactful and empowering.

"Bob, you did a great job at this morning's meeting. I appreciate how you let everyone talk, but kept the session from getting out of hand. You always seem to know how to balance fairness with efficiency."

Handwritten Equals Special

If you really want someone to feel the full weight of your compliment, put it in writing as well. A good old-fashioned snail-mail letter or handwritten note shows a special effort on your part to express appreciation. It also gives the person a real life reminder of your praise.

Sincerity Adds Meaning

Compliments that mean the most come from people who say what they mean, and mean what they say. You can increase the impact of your complements by only passing on praise when you sincerely feel it. In part, this means being honest enough to say when things aren't working so well. If the people you work with trust you to provide constructive criticism, they will also trust your positive compliments as genuine and authentic.

Turnaround Is Fair Play

If you are lucky enough to be on the receiving end of a compliment, learn to accept it with grace. Many people feel embarrassed when complimented and stumble and stammer in the face of appreciation. Don't. Let the other person have the satisfaction of giving you a sincere compliment. When all else fails, simply saying thank you will always suffice.

Provide Empathy

When most people deal with a customer (or coworker) who is upset, angry, or frustrated, they listen with an agree/disagree point of view. In other words, as the person is talking, they weigh what the other person is saying and, more importantly, feeling, against how valid, true, or reasonable they consider his or her response to be.

Invariably, this way of listening creates conflict when what the customer is feeling, and what you think they should be feeling, do not match. Empathetic listening helps move you away from conflict and towards accepting the customer's emotional point-of-view without necessarily agreeing with the content of what they say. Here are some helpful hints at how to be more empathetic:

Use Empathetic Phrases

Customers want to know that you understand their point of view and feelings regardless of whether you agree with them or not. Empathetic phrases that convey this include:

- I understand your point of view.
- I can see why you would feel that way.
- I hear what you are saying.
- I'm sorry that happened.

Make Reflective Statements

A reflective statement is an educated guess about what you think the customer is feeling or thinking. These statements work the best when they are phrased as a soft observation, rather than a hard fact. Examples include:

- It sounds like...
- It seems like...
- Would it be correct to say...

Paraphrase

Saying back to your customers—in your own words—the essence of what they have conveyed to you, lets them know that you have heard their concerns. It also gives your customer the opportunity to correct, on the spot, any misunderstandings. Good paraphrase starters include:

- What I hear you saying is...
- In other words...
- Let me see if I understand...

These three methods for expressing empathy go a long way to helping your customer feel heard, de-escalating angry situations, and cooling down a brewing crisis. By using these techniques you stay busy trying to understand your customer's concerns and circumstances, rather than focusing on your own point of view.

Raise Questions

Asking the right questions at the right time is essential to effective problem solving. Two types of question are useful in gathering information—open- and close-ended.

Open-ended questions, by their nature, invite the customer to give you additional information beyond a one or two word answer. They usually begin with words such as how, why, what, who, which, when, and where. Examples of good open-ended phrases to carry in your customer service toolbox include:

- What kind of information/product/service are you looking for?
- How do you want to use this product/service/information?
- How did this problem arise?
- Where else have you looked?

The advantage of open-ended questions is that they encourage the customer to give you an unrestricted response, they are perceived as less threatening and they help develop trust. Keep in mind that you need to allow for a bit more talking time when you ask an open-ended question.

Closed-ended questions usually evoke short or single-word answers. They are more leading and restrictive than open-ended questions and begin with do, does, is, are, have, has, can, will, and would. A few examples include:

- Is that correct?
- Do you approve?
- Does that answer the question?
- Would you like any more information?

The advantage of closed-ended questions is that they are quick and to the point, requiring less time for exploration and discussion. However when closed-ended questions are used exclusively, they can lead to incomplete information. They also hinder the customer from expressing his or her feelings and point of view—a necessary ingredient in creating rapport.

Take a look at the example below and notice how you might respond differently to being asked each of these questions—one open, one closed.

Open-ended question:
What happened when you tried to return the puppy?
Closed-ended version:
Do you have a receipt for the puppy?

Recover From Service Blunders

No company in the world can satisfy *all* of its customers *all* of the time. Even the most highly regarded service stars make mistakes. Their secret is service recovery. They know that when mistakes happen, the trick is to restore their customers confidence and win back their respect right away, or chance them never returning.

In fact, if you resolve a customer's problem quickly, the likelihood of them repurchasing from you is a monstrous 82 percent. If you don't resolve their problem, that number goes down to a miniscule 19 percent.

Recovery is one of the low hanging fruits on the service tree. It's relatively inexpensive (it costs six times more to gain a new customer than to retain a current one) and easy to implement. The three steps to recovery are:

1. Apologize.
2. Fix the problem.
3. Offer a recovery token.

Apologize

Regardless of who's at fault, be willing to say I'm sorry. An apology isn't necessarily an admission of guilt, but can be an acknowledgement of the inconvenience and stress caused by the problem. For example:

- "I'm sorry that happened."
- "I apologize for the inconvenience this has caused."

- "I'm sorry we made this mistake."
- "I'd like to apologize on behalf of our company."

The expression "The customer is always right" may not be true—sometimes they are wrong. But they *are* always your customers.

Fix the Problem

An apology without a fix is a hollow gesture. Once you're aware of the customer's problem, your job is to rectify the situation as quickly and easily as possible. Often a simple solution presents itself. For example:

- Revise an invoice.
- Change an order.
- Waive a fee.
- Replace a defective product.
- Resend a form.
- Express mail.

At other times, however, fixing the problem requires more effort and expense. At these times, a give-and-take conversation with the customer is necessary to work out a solution that is acceptable to everyone.

Offer a Recovery Token

Apologizing and fixing the customer's problem scores big points, but to hit a home run, give the customer a recovery token. A recovery token is an action you take to make up for mistakes made. For example:

> *One car dealership on the east coast makes a habit of calling every customer after they have come in for service to see how satisfied they are. If they are dissatisfied, the dealership goes right over, picks up the car, fixes it, washes it, details it, and delivers it back to the customer at no charge. Not surprisingly, the new customers they get from referrals more than covers the costs of their efforts.*

Other recovery tokens you can see everyday in business include:

- An airline gives you a free drink or movie certificate because the flight was delayed.

- A coffee shop buys you a non-fat, decaf cappuccino because your eggs come over hard, not easy.

- The magazine company extends your subscription by an extra six months, because they had your initial address wrong.

- The doctor's office sends you a hand-written card apologizing for forgetting to call your prescription into the pharmacy.

Redefine Your Service

Customers are constantly evaluating your company based on their own unique points of view and personal experiences. When you are lucky enough to get a peek inside their private thoughts about how you are doing, be careful not to fall into the trap of defensiveness by disagreeing or disbelieving what they are telling you. Remember, for all intents and purposes, their perception is reality. For example:

> *The senior executives of a transportation company in New England were listening to the live feedback of a focus group taking place in the next room. Several large customers in the group explained how the company's billing process was cumbersome, inaccurate, and long in need of an overhaul. On hearing these remarks, the executives, in the privacy of their observation room next door, became agitated and began justifying to one another why the system didn't work and criticizing the customers' lack of understanding.*

Knowing exactly how your customers assess you is vital for re-defining service that fires on all cylinders. For example, a restaurant that prides itself on cleanliness and good food misses the customer boat if the servers are impolite and the meals come out late. Regardless of your industry, customers use a three-part mental checklist to score your service.

Quality of Product

This is the tangible aspect of your service. In a restaurant, it's the freshness and flavor of the food; for an airline, it's the cleanliness of the cabin; for a Web designer, it is the look of the site they create; for an insurance broker, it's the features of the policy; and so on. It's true that customers expect a quality product at a competitive price, and this is often the initial reason they choose to do business with your company. However, if this is all you offer, it's all to easy for a competitor to steal your customers away.

Ease of Procedures

Once captured by your remarkable product, the customer moves on to the next item on their mental checklist: procedures. These are the systems and processes that your clients must go through to get the product or service you offer. The best web designer in the world won't get customer referrals if she keeps missing deadlines and making her customer wait. Airlines know that a clean, modern aircraft means little if they have a terrible on-time record. And who cares if the insurance agent has secured you low auto insurance premiums if the insurance company takes six months to pay for a fender bender repair?

The Personal Touch

The third item on your customer's mental checklist includes the attitudes, actions, and behaviors you show to your customers. No matter how good your product and how efficient your procedures, your personal rapport (friendliness, responsiveness, caring and courtesy, and so on) can make the difference between spectacular and mediocre service.

Customer Service In An Instant

Depending on your industry and the particulars of your business, all three items on the checklist are not necessarily created equal. In some situations, your customers value one or two above another. For example a four-star hotel that has bright, clean rooms with great views (product) can lose customers if checking-in is disorganized and takes forever (procedure). Alternatively, your local fast-food chain knows that server friendliness (personal) is far less important than how long you have to wait for your ChubbyBurger (product).

Exercise

Think about your company's service. Using a scale of 1–10 (1=Awful, 10=Outstanding) how would you rate your customers perception of each of these three items on the checklist.

Product_____   Procedure_____   Personal_____

Do your customers consider all three areas equally important? If not, which are the most important? Are your scores consistent with this?

If you have any scores lower than seven, you have some work to do. What actions could you take to help improve this area?

Reframe Your Outlook

Do you see the glass as half empty or half full? Reframing is a powerful personal tool you have for shifting your perspective in almost any situation. It is not pretending everything is okay when it isn't. It is recognizing that there are a variety of lenses you can view a situation through, some more empowering to than others.

For example: One of your favorite coworkers, to whom you have been close for years, announces that she is leaving the company to take an exciting job in China. Sure you're happy for her, but your also sad she is leaving and annoyed that the boss has asked you to formally take on the job of hiring and training her replacement. A few days later, when you have mulled over the situation, you realize that having the chance to hire and train the new person is an opportunity for you—one where you can grow and learn. You will miss your friend, but are suddenly excited about this new project. In essence, you have reframed the situation from one of annoyance to one of opportunity.

The following three steps will serve you well when you are in any situation where you feel pressured, stressed, or annoyed and want to reframe.

Step 1: Fix What You Can

It's the day before a big budget meeting and you are a nervous wreck.

What specifically is causing you discomfort? The answer may be that you need more information about a certain line item, or you may need to get more familiar with a particular reporting procedure. If there is an action you can take to relieve the source of your stress, then do it.

Step 2: Identify Your Negative Thinking Patterns

Now that you have fixed what you can, there may still be circumstances beyond your control that are causing you stress. The goal is to change how you "think" about those.

Let's say you view your boss as an *uptight*, *chronic micro-manager*, who *always* nit picks every last detail, *every* time you have a *stupid* budget meeting.

Notice how this way of thinking is loaded with negative labels, exaggerations, and generalizations. All placed on top of the hard and fast fact that your boss asks a lot of detailed questions in budget meetings—period.

While his/her asking questions may be stressful enough, these thinking patterns create additional stress that we know you can live without.

Consider a situation you currently find stressful at work. What are the negative thinking patterns you have associated with it?

Step 3: Create a New Perspective

A lot of the stress you experience in the previous example is tied to your perception of your manager's behavior, rather than the meeting itself. Every situation—especially difficult ones—have more than one interpretation. To complete the reframing process, choose a perspective that helps resolve the situation rather than exacerbate it.

For example, in the previous scenario you could interpret your manager's behavior as being a pain in the assets, or you could drop the negative thinking patterns and interpret it as your boss's commitment to fiscal integrity and finding any problems sooner, rather than later, in the budgeting process. Which interpretation creates more or less stress?

Thinking about the situation you currently find stressful at work, invent a few new interpretations that you would find less stressful.

Respect the Power Player

People with this style always have their eyes on the prize and know exactly how they are going to get there (think Donald Trump). They are results-oriented, good at managing tasks, and like to win. Tell-tale signs of a Power Player include:

- Direct eye contact.
- Quick movements.
- Fast and forceful speech.
- Direct and down-to-earth, bottom-line language.
- Quick decision making.
- Pressuring others to make quick decisions.
- Working independently or directing others.
- Abrupt in tone.

- Competitive nature.
- Focus on tangible results.

The strength of those with this style is their ability to make quick decisions. They are high achievers who know how to lead themselves and others in a single-minded fashion towards the goals and objectives they have set. Willing to take risks, they often reap the rewards. Because they are strong willed and work well independently, they prosper in positions of authority and are often found among the ranks of CEOs, lawyers, and politicians.

The downside is that under stress and pressure, Power Players move too quickly and overlook critical details. When up against the wall, they may override their own or others feelings to get the job done. If their hard working, competitive nature goes into overdrive, they can become autocratic and attacking—alienating staff and coworkers.

Exercise:

To get more familiar with this style, think of someone you know who might have a Power Player style and answer the questions that follow.

Do they have a relatively high degree of assertiveness and a low degree of emotional expression?

What behaviors have you observed that indicate they have this style?

What do you admire about this person's style?

With what do you have trouble?

Rev Up Your Recognition

A recent survey of 4 million Americans by the Gallup Organization showed that 65 percent of workers receive no recognition for a job well done, an alarming statistic, considering that recognition not only improves retention but also performance and morale. According to a Wichita State University study, the top five non-cash motivators are:

- Personally congratulating employees who do a good job.
- Writing personal notes about good performance.
- Using performance as the basis for promotion.
- Publicly recognizing employees for good performance.
- Holding morale-building meetings to celebrate successes.

Revving up your recognition quotient can be easy and inexpensive. Use the following who, what, where, and when questions to plan your strategy.

Who?

Who do you want to recognize? Fairness works better than favoritism, so don't be stingy with your appreciation. Make acknowledgment a regular practice that includes *everyone*, rather than a rare event for the privileged few.

What?

Be specific. Throwaway phrases such as "good job" and "thanks a lot" are too mundane to have lasting impact. Make your appreciation count by giving a short detailed description of what attitude/behavior is being recognized. For example, "I want to thank you for all the extra work you have put in this month. I know it hasn't been easy, but your great attitude and willingness to work longer hours has made a difficult time easier for all of us. Thank you."

Where?

Recognition means more if it happens in a casual-yet-organized way. For example, going to the person's cubicle works better than shouting an "attaboy" at them as you rush past them down the hallway.

When?

Find a time when you are most likely to have the other's persons full attention. For example: Expressing appreciation when the recipient is on a tight deadline, swallowed up in a huge project, will waste your kind words.

Motivating Moves

Offering cash is tempting, but it generally takes five to eight percent of an employee's salary to change behavior if the reward is dollars. While words are the heart of a sincere appreciation, offering a tangible non-cash reward reinforces and deepens your message. Non-cash awards should match the achievement you are honoring. For example:

Send a letter of praise from a senior executive.	Bring in cookies.
Write a handwritten note.	Give a plant or flowers.
Name a program after your employees.	Tickets to a sporting event.
	Gift certificates.
Buy balloons.	Dinner for two.
	Time off with pay.

Change job titles.

Service pins.

Highlight in newsletter.

Free 15-minute massage at work.

Training retreat.

Temporary parking space.

Staff t-shirts.

Music CD.

iTunes gift certificate.

Personalized Post-its.

Say "I," Not "You"

One way to head off potential conflict is to get into the habit of framing your not-so-easy to say feelings (usually anger, frustration, sadness, irritation, and so on) as "I" statements rather than "you" statements. "I" statement focus on *your* feelings, avoid accusations and help de-escalate tension. For example, which of the following makes you feel more defensive:

"You never call me back when you say you are going to. You're really frustrating to work with."

or...

"When you promise you'll call me back and you don't, I feel frustrated."

This first example implies blame, encouraging the listener to, in turn, blame the speaker back. "You" statements assign fault and encourage the recipient to deny wrongdoing. For example, if you say, "You never call me back when you say you are going to," the likely response will be, "No, I don't," or "That's not true." Then you reply with "Yes, you do." And on and on it goes. This leads to an argument that takes you further away from solving the problem and closer to conflict.

In the second response, the speaker simply stated the problem from her point of view—without blaming the other person. This strategy allows the other person to partner with you in finding a solution and save face at the same time.

Take the "Think" Test

To easily determine if the "I" statement you are about to express is really a feeling, and not an opinion disguised as a feeling, try the "think" test. Imagine you plan on telling your coworker Albert in accounting...

"I feel like you are being a real jerk when you don't replace the ink cartridge in the printer."

Now substitute the word "think" for "feel" as in...

"I think you are being a real jerk when you don't replace the ink cartridge in the printer."

In this case "think" and "feel" are interchangeable—what you are expressing is a thought, not a feeling. If you try to coach negative opinions as feelings, even in the guise of an "I" statement, the other person will still feel attacked.

On the other hand, if one word can't be substituted for another, you are probably conveying a feeling. For example:

"I feel irritated when I go to use the printer, and you have not replaced the ink cartridge."

The sentence "I think irritated whenever I go to use the printer..." doesn't make any sense—so you are more than likely expressing a feeling.

Say No With Style

If you noticed this sign on the wall of your local photocopy shop, what impression would you get?

"A lack of planning on your part does not constitute an emergency on mine."

Do you think they would they bend over backwards to give you what you want? Probably not. While no one likes to hear that they can't have what they want, when they want it, and it's impossible to make no sound like yes, the key is to avoid giving your customers a "hard no."

A "hard no" is the customer equivalent of hitting a brick wall and offers no solutions, alternatives, or empathy. When you give the customer a 'hard no' *you* become the barrier to what they want. The result is annoyance, anger, and a sudden strong desire to get around the wall any way possible—often by going over it to your boss.

The next time your customer asks for the impossible, instead of responding with a hard no such as, "That's not our policy," "I can't do that," or "you can't do that," flip into a "soft no" state of mind and use these simple, but life-saving phrases:

"What I will do is..." and "What you can do is..."

The first phrase helps shift you away from what you *can't* do to what you *can*, and moves the conversation in a more positive direction. The key is to fulfill other needs and propose alternative ways the customer might get his or her problem solved. The second phrase includes the customer in the solution. Here's an example of a hard no converted to a soft one:

Irritated Customer:	*"I know the part I want is back ordered, but can't you just take one that is slotted for another customer and give it to me instead?"*
Supplier, using a "hard no":	*"That's against our policy."*
Supplier, using a soft "no":	*"What I will do is contact another supplier and see if they have the part in stock. What you can do is give us permission to use expedited shipping if we manage to locate it."*

Even though the alternative may not be the customer's first choice, the offer of a soft no, versus a hard no, helps create good will and saves stress all around!

Exercise:

Think of a situation in which you routinely need to say no to your customers:

What would be a typical hard no statement in that situation? Using the two phrases below, convert this hard no into a soft no:

What I will do is:

What you can do is:

Set Expectations on the Spot

All sorts of factors outside of your control—including sales material, company policy, previous experiences, and personal style—contribute to your customer's expectations. The only expectations you control are the ones you set and manage.

One way to do this is to give realistic deadlines for the delivery of service, products, and information. Too often in your enthusiasm to give customers what they want (or for fear of making them mad), you may find yourself promising something that may be hard to deliver. This type of *over promising and under delivering* leads to loss of credibility and unhappy customers whose expectations have not been fulfilled. For example:

- The announcement on the phone says, "Wait time is five minutes," but, in reality, it takes the customer 10 minutes to reach a real live person.

- The service provider tells the customer to expect the package within seven days. It takes two weeks to arrive.

- The nurse makes a 2 p.m. appointment with the patient. They don't get in to see the doctor until 3 p.m.

- The airline representative announces that the flight will depart an hour late at 10:30 a.m. At 11 a.m., it is announced that the flight will be delayed until noon.

Customer Service In An Instant

The solution is to get into the habit of *under promising and over delivering*. This involves building a "safety padding" into your time line for unforeseen problems and emergencies. For example:

> *A sales representative at a catalog company knows that she can get the customer's "pink piggy slippers" order to her within three business days. However, the representative tells the customer that the "pink piggies" will be delivered within four business days. By creating a four-day rather than a three-day delivery expectation, the catalog company will over deliver on its promise and the customer will be delighted that the order has arrived a day earlier than planned.*

This habit works great with coworkers as well. Nothing builds teamwork faster than consistently keeping your promises with the people with whom you work.

Once you are engaged with the customer, even if things seem to be going well, it's a good idea to monitor the customers changing satisfaction level. Even during the course of a single conversation a customer's satisfaction level can increase or decrease. Ask yourself if the customers' satisfaction seems to be changing for better or worse.

If your customer's satisfaction level seems to be going up, notice what they are responding to and do more of it. If his or her level of satisfaction seems to be decreasing, ask yourself, what happened and what can you do to reverse it?

Finally, reverse the situation by making sure your customer knows what specific information and actions you need to help you help him or her.

Strengthen Service Habits

Banker, architect, sales assistant, office manager—no matter what your field, your customers have a lot in common: they all want to be treated well. Here are the basic habits for universally keeping customers happy.

Keep Your Word

The poet Robert Service wrote, "A promise made is a debt unpaid." Nothing can undermine your credibility faster than not doing what you said you would do, when you said you would do it. For example: Always call a customer back by the time you promised—even if it's to say that you don't yet have the information they want and you'll get back to him or her again later. In this day and age, when customers anticipate poor follow-up, keeping your word can wow them!

Be on Time

If you have a conference call, business lunch, or staff meeting, showing up on time is a statement of respect. The main reason for running behind is lack of planning, so use the following checklist to beat the clock:

____ Honestly assess how much time it will take you to prepare for the meeting. Include the time you will need to gather materials, write an outline, Google travel directions, and so on.

_____ If the meeting is in another location, add in travel time and be sure to give yourself a few extra minutes for traffic jams, parking, and such.

_____ Total your prep and travel time and add a few extra minutes for wrapping things up at the office.

_____ Lastly, set an alarm/calendar alert to go off at your calculated departure time. When the alarm goes off, don't negotiate with yourself to squeeze out a few extra minutes. It's this discipline that guarantees an on-time arrival.

Go the Extra Mile

Make going out of your way for your customers a habit. By doing small, extra things for them, your service is remembered and your company differentiates itself from its competitors. On those occasions when you cannot go as far out of your way as your customers would like—and when you can't say yes and you have to say no—be sure that you get into the next habit.

Present Alternatives

Sometimes circumstances beyond your control (out of stock, against company policy, and so on) make it impossible to give your customers what they're asking for.

Whatever the reason, reduce their disappointment and increase their satisfaction by presenting alternatives that can help solve the problem in some other way. For example:

"I'm sorry we no longer stock the Ninety-Six Inch Super Candles, but I can recommend two Forty-Eight Inchers. They can be stacked one on top of the other."

"Unfortunately, we are prohibited by federal regulations from receiving your check via the fax. I can process a credit card over the phone."

"I'm sorry we can't install a hot tub in your apartment building. Have you considered replacing your bathtub with a Whirly-Relaxer Jet Spa?

Treat Your Customer as the Most Important Part of Your Job

When all the functions of your job—meetings, paperwork, telephone calls, and so on—start to get you down, develop the habit of changing your attitude. Viewing your customers as interruptions to the work that you have to get done is all too easy. By focusing on your customers as the reason why you do your job, you will make them feel important. After all, ultimately, they are the ones who write your paycheck.

Ditch Your Bad Habits

The habits outlined above are all the good habits, but what if you have some bad customer service habits that you want to eliminate? Following are three simple ideas:

- After you realize you have fallen back on the bad habit, think about what you could have done differently.
- If you catch yourself in the middle of acting out the bad habit, stop and try something else.
- Just before you are about to fall prey to the bad habit, stop yourself and pick a better action.

Style Step

You have the ability to access the strengths of all the working styles to more or less of a degree. Practicing style stepping gives you a chance to exercise and emphasize these less frequently used aspects of yourself. As a general rule, keep in mind the following when dealing with each of the four different working styles:

With Power Players: These action-oriented individuals like to get down to business straight away. Don't waste their time with chitchat, hesitation, or rambling. Make your points clear, strong, and brief—even if it's during a two-minute conversation in the hallway. Follow up on any important meetings or discussions in writing and do what you say you're going to do, when you say you're going to do it. Quick tips include:

- Make direct eye contact.
- Maintain an erect posture.
- Speak relatively quickly.
- Focus on results.
- Use their time efficiently and honor all time limits.
- Be prepared and organized.

With Passionate Persuaders: These enthusiastic go-getters love pizzazz and are turned off by too much detail. Have important conversations with them by phone or face to face and skip the memos. When you do have to e-mail them make it brief, positive, and energetic. Showing excitement about their ideas, focusing on the big picture, and having fun when working together is key with this style. Quick tips include:

- Use relatively big arm/hand gestures.
- Speak fast, with energy and inflection.
- Ask about their intuitive take on things.
- Support your ideas with feedback from people they respect.
- Paraphrase agreements.
- Balance between fun and staying on track.

With People Pleasers: These feeling-oriented folks want to like others and be liked by them. Taking the time to chat about casual topics, family life and personal feelings will build rapport and pave the way for smoother problem solving. If you need to discuss a highly emotional topic, by all means do it face to face if possible. A handwritten thank you note will do wonders. Quick tips include:

- Maintain casual eye contact
- Speak softly and at a moderate pace
- Draw out their opinions
- Avoid countering their ideas with logic
- Encourage their expression of any doubts or fears
- Mutually agree on all goals, actions and dates

With Problem Solvers: These fact and figure lovers are open to hearing what you have to say, as long as it's presented in a logical, well-thought-out, and research-based way. Memos, e-mail, and written communication in general work well with this type. Avoid exaggeration and enthusiasm when presenting an idea. Instead lay out the pro's and con's as level-headed as possible. Quick tips include:

- Steer clear of big arm and hand gestures.
- Don't move around too much.
- Use a moderately paced tone of voice.
- Avoid speaking to loudly.
- Be more formal in your speech and manners.
- Be on time.
- Let them proceed at a deliberate and slow pace.

Switch Filters

Occasionally viewing customers and coworkers through negative filters is a fact of life. But learning to *switch* filters redirects your attention away from unhelpful perceptions (stupid, creepy, clueless, and so on) and refocuses your mind in a more positive direction. When you notice that you have a negative filter, you can slide it to the back of your brain by simply and silently asking yourself the question:

> *"What does this person need and how can
> I provide it to the best of my ability?"*

As soon as you ask yourself this question, you create a "Service Filter" that builds a pathway to constructively dealing with the customers' problems. By switching filters, you illuminate the issues that need to be addressed, rather than your personal feelings about the customer's behavior.

DIFFICULT
CUSTOMER

"What does this
person need and
how can I
provide it?"

Concern, empathy,
listening, helpfulness,
problem resolution

Switching filters doesn't mean that you need to give up your opinion. That may prove difficult—especially if you have known the person for along time or have had a particularly contentious conversation. However, switching filters, if only for the duration of the conversation, guarantees that you remain resourceful and keeps your stress level to a minimum.

126

Signs for a Switch

These tell-tale signs are a signal that you are listening through negative filter. When they show up, switch to a Service Filter:

- Rapid heart beat
- Sweaty palms
- Anxious when the phone rings
- Tight jaw, shoulders, or neck
- Headache
- Holding your breath
- Trembling or twitching

- Itchy skin
- Fatigue
- Butterflies in stomach
- Dry mouth
- Shallow breathing
- Impatience
- Irritation at the sound of the other person's voice

Temper Your
Telephone Tone

Nowhere is the phrase "it's not what you say, but how you say it" truer than when talking to customers. On the phone, your tone of voice accounts for 86 percent of how a customer perceives your attitude.

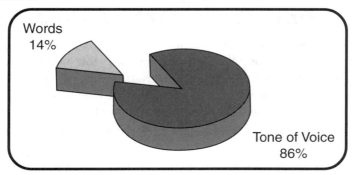

Words
14%

Tone of Voice
86%

Even if you say all the right words, if your tone is inconsistent with your lofty language, it is heard as insincere and shallow. Tweak your tone to perfection by trying out the following three things:

1. Modify Your Inflection

Inflection is the peaks and valleys in your tone when you speak. If you hang out down in the valleys (with a minimum amount of modulation) your voice will sound flat and monotone, giving the impression that you are indifferent and unconcerned. For example, think back to the last time you called a busy switchboard on a Monday afternoon. Chances are the person answering the phone was inflection-challenged, having said the same greeting three million times that day. Your voice will loose its oomph factor, unless you remember to add a few high tones in amid the lows.

On the other hand, intensely jumping back and forth from extreme valleys to extreme peaks—like a crazed DJ from your local pop radio station—sounds superficial and insincere. For example, think back to the last time you were interrupted at dinnertime by an overly-bubbly telemarketer who greeted you like a long-lost buddy. Do you hang up or have a chat?

Good inflection is having a reasonable amount of highs and lows in your tone so that you sound interested and animated. Think about how you might read a story to a child, to keep their interest.

Exercise:
Find Your Perfect Pitch

To find your perfect inflection level, say the following phrase out loud three times: the first time say it with low inflection (the valleys), the second time say it with too much inflection (the peaks), the third time, adjust your inflection so that it feels comfortable and rests somewhere between the extremes of the first two.

"We have a new product that I think you're going to like."

2. Adjust Your Speed

Some people naturally speak fast and others more slowly, depending on style, circumstances, and geography. As a service provider your job is to put the customer at ease by approximately matching their rate of speech. For example, if you are from New York and your customer is from Texas, there's a good chance that one of you will be talking a lot faster than the other. As the New Yorker, you would slow down (and resist the urge to finish the customer's sentences). By cooling your heels and giving the customer enough time to say what they need, you help create instant rapport. If the geography is reversed (you are from Texas and your customer is from New York), picking up your speed would close the geographic divide and strengthen the relationship.

Slowing down your speed is also important when you are working with a customer who is confused or disoriented. The average American speaks at a rate of 100 to 150 words per minute. But, confused customers listen at a much slower rate, so they miss more of what you are saying. Slowing down also saves you from having to repeat yourself.

3. Vary Your Volume

When customers are upset they tend to speak louder than normal. This is one situation in which matching the customer's tone is a big mistake. Raising your voice adds more fuel to the fire and can start a shouting match. Instead, put out the flames by reducing your volume. This encourages the customer to dial down their level to meet yours.

Speaking louder to a customer *is* a good approach if they are confused and need guidance. The raised tone keeps their attention on you and gives you more control over the conversation.

Tone Temperatures

Tone of voice comes in three temperatures: warm, medium, and cold.

Warm tones express your sincerity, friendliness, concern, and helpfulness.

Medium tones are neither friendly nor unfriendly. They make the statement that you are just doing your job, and are emotionally detached.

A cold tone of voice expresses disinterest, boredom, anger, and frustration.

To hear this for yourself, try saying the following sentence out loud. Say it three times, once with a warm tone, the second time with a medium tone and the third time with a cold tone. Notice how your inflection, speed, and volume change with each temperature.

"Are you aware that your payment is overdue?"

Think Through Outsourcing

In today's global marketplace, outsourcing to overseas call centers is business as usual. Viewed as a way to lower costs and boost profits, outsourcing can sometimes create as many problems as it solves. A 2005 Gartner study predicted that 60 percent of organizations that outsource a part of their customer service process will encounter customer attrition and concealed costs that outweigh potential savings.

While there is no magic formula to determining whether outsourcing customer service functions is right for your company, before you jump onto the bandwagon, consider how compatible outsourcing is with your business philosophy, goals, and customer-service objectives. Ask yourself:

Are we doing this just to avoid the expense and effort of creating a call center? Keep in mind that outsourcing a call center requires a great deal of planning and ongoing management. Considering the whole picture, what are the *real* benefits you will gain? What are *real* costs?

What is the scope of outsourcing? Will the outsourcer take all customer calls; overflow calls from our in-house call center, or specific calls that require less technical knowledge? For example, a computer company might outsource sales calls from its catalog, but answer technical support inquiries in-house.

Have we defined service levels and standards for the outsourcer? Don't leave the care of your customers up to the goodwill and promises of the outsourcer. Instead, do your research and find out how long your customers are willing to wait for an e-mail response or hold in a telephone queue. Create service standards consistent with your research and contractually make your vendor adhere to them.

Are we willing and able to review call center reports? Reviewing service levels and complaint logs is a valuable part of call center activity, and not one that you want to lose sight of in an outsourcing arrangement.

Is the vendor experienced in your industry? You want outsourcers who understand your field, be it catalog sales, healthcare systems, financial advice and so on. Outsourcers who know the business of your business are essential for satisfying customer's questions and concerns.

Pros and Cons

With more than $12 billion a year being spent on outsourcing worldwide, it remains a popular option to in-house customer support. At the same time, a backlash is occurring and some companies are bringing their customer contact back in house. Here are the major pros and cons to consider.

Pros

In the event of a new product launch, an overwhelming amount of customer service calls can come in. Outsourcing eliminates the problem of having to bring a large group of new employees up to speed to handle the situation.

If you are at the point where answering customer calls would require a large capital investment in CRM software, telephone systems, and so on, outsourcing can be a definite cost savings.

For a smaller business, outsourcing may be a good way to jump-start your call center, until you have the capital and experience to bring it in house.

Cons

In order to keep costs of outscoring lower, overseas outsourcers are more likely to spend less on training staff in customer service skills.

The outsourcer's staff probably won't have a personal relationship with your company or identify with overall company goals. Hence, promoting the positive reputation of your company may not be a top priority for them.

There is a high risk of cultural misunderstandings due to language and accent problems.

Treat Your Colleagues as Customers

There is an old adage that says, "If you are not serving the customer, your job is to serve someone who does." In a customer focused company, everyone *knows* they are responsible for "internal" service. Internal customer service occurs anytime you or one of your colleagues needs products, information, or service from another person or department within the company. For example:

- Your coworker in accounting e-mails requesting your recent expense report, so she can close out the month on time.

- Your colleague in the next cubical asks if you can cover his phone for the next hour while he is away at a dental appointment.

- Your peer in production asks for contact information on your client.

- Your office mate walks into your office and says, "I really need your help."

It's easy, in the face of too much to do, to view internal customers as an interruption of your *real* job. But just stop and think about where you would be and how much harder your job would become, without the cooperation of your peers. As you go through this book, whenever you hear or see the word "customer," remember you can substitute the word "coworker" and apply all the same skills and techniques.

Ultimately, the way you serve internal customers also affects the service your paying customers receive. For example:

The customer calls the production department and asks you for information that you need to get from the sales department. You contact the sales department, and your coworker quickly and politely provides the details you desire. You then, in turn, can quickly get back to the customer and provide him or her with a high level of service.

This, of course, is a scenario from the perfect work world and is not always the way things play out in reality. What would happen if you contact the sales department and your colleague tells you (abruptly) that he does not have the time to help you? Now what? Your coworker's attitude and lack of action directly impacts your ability to service your customer, even though your colleague has no direct contact with him or her. The quality of service customers receive is, to a large degree, dependant on the internal customer service within that company.

Customer Service In An Instant

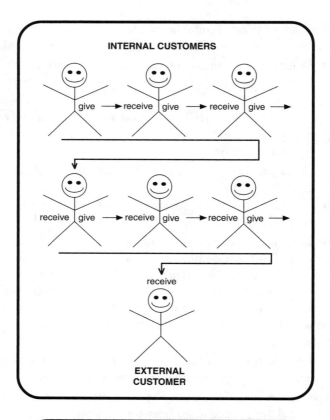

Spend Time Sharing

When employees from different parts of the company spend time together, they not only get to know each other better personally, but their desire and willingness to provide internal service increases. The forums for this type of sharing can be casual lunch get-togethers or formal task teams. Either way, giving employees the opportunity to swap information, brainstorm problem solutions, and discuss work situations will go a long way to breaking down department walls and staving off turf wars.

Tune Up Your Telephone Etiquette

You never get a second chance to make a first impression. Something as straightforward as a telephone call, for example, can make or break your service reputation. Consider the following all-too-familiar phone phrases and notice how, in fewer than 10 seconds, a bad service moment is born:

- You'll have to hold.
- He's not here now—try later.
- You have reached the wrong department—call back.

When it comes to phone customer service, a little etiquette goes a long way. Take a few minutes to test your etiquette IQ and then bring your telephone manners up to speed by using the guidelines below.

Answering the Phone

The time is 3:45 p.m., and Jeremy is putting the final touches on his PowerPoint presentation. The phone rings, and he ignores the first three rings and on the fourth picks up and says "Good afternoon, this is Jeremy, how may I help you?" Jeremy is demonstrating good telephone etiquette, true or false?

True and false. Jeremy has done a good job of setting the tone by giving a greeting, saying his name, and offering to help. However, he let the phone ring four times before picking it up. The maximum amount of time the phone should ring before being answered is three.

Basic Etiquette Primer

- Give a correct greeting.
- Identify your company or department.
- Identify yourself.
- Offer to help.
- Answer you phone live (vs. voicemail) at least some of the time.
- Answer calls within three rings.

Taking a Message

Kele is the assistant to the V.P. of marketing for a toy manufacturer. She receives a call asking if her boss is available. "I'm sorry he is out at a meeting," Kele says "May I ask who's calling?" The customer provides a name and Kele replies, "He should be back this afternoon. Can I take a message or can I help you with something?" Kele is demonstrating good telephone etiquette, true or false?

True. Kele got it right by letting the caller know the status of her boss's availability before asking for their name. When you ask a customers name first, they feel screened.

Basic Etiquette Primer

- Explain your coworker's absence in a positive light.
- Inform the caller of availability before you ask their name.
- Give an estimated time of your coworker's return.
- Write down all important information and attach any pertinent notes.

Putting Callers On Hold

Shirley is a sales assistant at a shoe store. Her supervisor, Norm, is having a brief meeting with her about some sexy new sneakers that have just arrived. Shirley's telephone rings. She immediately picks it up, greets the customer, and says, "Let me put you on hold for just a moment." Shirley is demonstrating good telephone etiquette, true or false?

False. In this scenario, Shirley did not ask the customer for his permission to hold, she told him.

Basic Etiquette Primer

- Ask the caller for his/her permission to hold and wait for a response.
- Tell the caller why they are being put on hold.
- If longer than one minute, set a time frame for how long you will be gone.
- Thank the caller for holding *before* you put them on hold.
- Return to the line every minute or within the established time frame.
- Thank the caller for holding upon returning to the line.

Transferring Calls

Jennifer works in the travel department of a large advertising agency. Her specialty is domestic travel. Her phone rings, and on the line is a coworker who needs help booking an overseas business trip to China. Jennifer says, "I'm sorry, I only deal with domestic travel, you need to talk to Bruce in international. Would you like me to transfer you?" Jennifer is demonstrating good telephone etiquette, true or false?

True. Jennifer was a shining example of how to transfer a call. She explained why she was not able to help, told the caller who they needed to speak with, and offered to transfer the call with permission.

Basic Etiquette Primer

- Inform the caller why he/she is being transferred.
- Ask the caller for permission to transfer them.
- Offer to take a message if the caller does not want to be transferred.

- Make sure that the party receiving the transfer is available to receive the call.
- Inform the party receiving the transfer of the caller's name and problem.

Turn Service Into Sales

Today, the job of a telephone customer-service representative (call center, technical support, or help desk) involves more than the passive handling of in-coming phone calls. Many companies are asking their service reps to do more than just respond to client problems, but to also go beyond and practice proactive sales. You have the opportunity to apply this type of cross-selling when a product or service your company offers could fulfill a client's immediate need or prevent a future problem.

If you find yourself shaking your head, throwing up your hands, and saying "But I'm just not a salesperson," think again. The skills required to be a killer customer service representative are a great foundation for being a service-oriented sales person. You can easily expand your value to both your company and your customer by learning how to *softly* offer additional products or services that would benefit your customer. Below are two key techniques for turning incoming service calls into sales opportunities.

Attention-Grabbers

In all likelihood, your customer has called you for assistance in resolving a problem, and helping them find a solution is your number-one concern. At some point, it may become clear to you that another product or service your company offers might be appropriate to mention. How do you do this? One of the best ways is to grab your customer's attention by using one of these five sentence-starters:

1. Make a general statement that relates to the client's business or problem. For example: "You know, our *Web Wise In An Instant* suite of products would allow you to develop programs much more quickly and efficiently."

2. Make a dramatic statement that relates to your client's business or problem. For example: "I'm looking at your account and you could have saved as much as $20,000 last quarter by switching to our *Gold Level* service plan."

3. Mention a known industry problem or concern. For example: "You're not alone. The last survey we did concluded that 40 percent of businesses in your industry are facing this problem. We have developed a new database system to help alleviate the trouble."

4. Use a third party reference to establish credibility for your product or service. For example: "The Wall Street Journal just ran an article on our latest upgrade and said it was the best in the industry."

Benefit Statements

Once you have peaked your customer's interest with an attention grabbing statement, a conversation will often follow about the product. This is the time to ask questions about the customer's needs and introduce a benefit statement.

A feature is a fact about your product or service. For example: "Our company's software education seminars are widely available across the United States."

A benefit tells the customer what value they will receive. It answers the question, "What is in it for me?" "We provide you with easy access to expert training on our software, as opposed to having to educate yourself or hire a private trainer. This saves you time and money."

A benefit statement clearly connects the customer's need with the features and benefits of your product or service. For Example: "Mr. Jones, I know you're concerned with getting all your staff up to speed on our new products. As you know, our education programs are widely available across the United States. That will not only facilitate this, but save you travel costs as well."

Exercise:

1. List one major feature (fact) about the product or service you sell.

2. For this feature, list at least one benefit, from the customer's point of view.

3. Put together a benefit statement that addressed the customer's need, mentions the feature, and stresses the benefit.

Understand the Problem Solver

People with this style usually focus more on facts than feelings and take an analytical, rather than emotional, view of situations (think Bill Gates). They are objective, practical, and know exactly what is expected of them. Tell tale signs of a Problem Solver include:

- Minimal facial expression.
- Controlled body movement with slow gestures.

- Tendency towards monotone with little inflection.
- Slow decision-making, after doing careful research.
- Language that is precise and focuses on specific details.
- Disciplined about time.
- Choosing words carefully.
- Expressing ideas tentatively and qualifying them.
- Risk averse.
- Serious in mood and affect.

The strength of those with this style lies in their willingness to take the time to examine the details of a situation in order to come up with a logical solution. Problem Solvers believe in doing things right the first time, so they don't have to be done over. They can work independently, and as such they are well-suited to the finance, science, and computer fields.

The downside of this style is that they often place analysis and accuracy ahead of other's feelings. Under stress they can over analyze in order to avoid making a decision. Because Problem Solvers are uncomfortable with feelings, they may avoid expressing strong emotions, even when this would be the best course of action.

Exercise:

To get more familiar with this style, think of someone you know who might have a Problem Solver style and answer the questions that follow.

Do they have a relatively low degree of assertiveness and a relatively low degree of emotional expression?

What behaviors have you observed that indicate they have this style?

What do you admire about this person's style?

What do you have trouble with?

Upgrade Your Influence

In the movie *Broadcast News*, actress Holly Hunter plays a producer who is confronted when she questions her bosses decision. Attempting to put her in her place, he scowls and says "It must be nice to always be the smartest person in the room."

"No" she replies, a pained expression on her face, "It's awful."

It can be frustrating when you want to share your perspective on a project or problem with those around you, but don't want your input to be intrusive, undervalued, or unwelcome. This is where your ability to assert your influence comes into play. To win over customers and influence coworkers, try out the following strategies:

Do: Make a direct request   Don't: Put forth a vague desire

When it comes to influencing others, asking for a specific result works better than putting forth a weak wish. Before you set out to capture the other person's heart and mind, be crystal clear about what specific outcomes you are looking to achieve.

Do: Ask questions   Don't: Just state opinions

Opinions, especially if they are positioned too strongly, can be polarizing, causing others to dig in their heels and defend their points of view. Instead, foster discussion by asking probing questions to understand their perspectives on the situation. In the end, the solution may not be the one you had in mind, but, nonetheless, a result that is in the best interests of all parties involved.

Do: Communicate early on   Don't: Wait until late in the game

The more time, money, and emotion the other person has invested in going down a particular path, the more married to that course of action they are likely to be. The best time to make your influence felt is when things are still at the discussion stage.

Do: Practice persistence   Don't: Give up too soon

Even though you may not make much headway at first (some people take more time than others to process information), if you feel strongly about something, don't let rejection or resistance stop you from respectfully bringing up the issue again and again, if appropriate. Each time you revisit the matter, pay attention to the successes and failures in communicating your concerns and adjust your approach accordingly.

Do: Give and take   Don't: Insist on your way

You can't influence others if accepting your ideas is seen as a losing proposition. The best influence strategies are those that offer a win-win situation. Be prepared to compromise by letting the other person know how you can help them achieve their goals and objectives.

Do: Have high hopes   Don't: Expect the worst

In the face of frustration, it can be easy to throw up your hands and lower your expectations. Don't. By maintaining high expectations, you set the stage for excellence. Give others the benefit of the doubt and expect them to want things to work out just as smoothly, quickly, and profitably as you do.

Customer Service In An Instant

Do: Focus on key points   Don't: Focus on personality

Keep the conversation focused on the consequences of choosing one path over another, not the other person's skills, talents, or wisdom. What are the negative impacts of the plan as it now stands? What potential problems do you see? What concerns you?

Do: Put forth evidence   Don't: Rely on opinions alone

Offer examples and stories that illustrate how the path you are proposing has lead to success. Strengthen your case by using role models, case studies, and expert opinions to demonstrate what has worked before.

Do: Share success   Don't: Seek credit

Although it's nice to receive recognition, the point of influencing is to achieve your objective, not be hailed as a genius for coming up with the next great idea. If the person you are pitching ends up thinking your good idea was their great idea—so much the better.

Do: Follow up in writing   Don't: Drop the ball

To avoid losing momentum after a conversation, write a short e-mail or note, because details can get lost in the heat of the discussion. Thank the person for taking the time to consider your point of view and offer to be available to continue the dialogue.

Walk Your Talk

On any given day of the week, groups of executives and managers are gathered in classrooms across the country discussing the importance of customer service. Most agree that service excellence is paramount to business success, but many don't realize that the path to world-class customer service begins with their own attitude and approach.

The old adage "fish stinks from the head down" describes how management sets the cultural tone within the organization. There is no quicker way for a manager to bring a screeching halt to service than by promoting it with their negative words and disrespecting it with their actions. For example:

> *One multinational consumer products company had received dozens of complaints regarding the handling of telephone calls at their corporate headquarters. In particular, the complaints centered around people not picking up ringing telephones, not returning voicemail messages, and general discourtesy. In response, the senior management within corporate headquarters asked the Human Resources department to design a half-day training seminar on customer service to help resolve the problem.*
>
> *The HR department did so and invited all upper management to attend hoping to underline management's support for a new way of thinking and also provide the opportunity to train some of the worst offenders—the managers themselves! The clear response back from upper management was they did not have time to attend, and they were not the ones who*

needed it. This lack of participation from senior manage-
ment created a negative impression before the seminar had
even begun.

In the end, it is not what you say, but the actions you take, that inform your staff of your "real" priorities. By "walking the talk" you earn the right to ask your staff to make a commitment to customer service. You can be a role model of service by:

- Enthusiastically handling customer calls, meetings, and problems.
- Using good service skills when dealing with difficult customers.
- Avoiding negative talk about customers behind their back.
- Greet your staff in the morning with a friendly tone.
- Discuss how you feel with your staff, but don't vent all over them.
- Be open to new ideas, approaches, and service solutions.
- Celebrate noteworthy occasions such as birthdays, promotions, and weddings.
- Use proper telephone and e-mail etiquette.
- Make a point to thank your staff often for a job well done.
- Be generous with compliments to both staff and customers.
- Say what you mean and mean what you say.

Thought-Starters

1. Have we established an executive task team whose job it is to review the status of our service focus and to create a plan for its continued improvement?

2. Do we have specific long-range goals for improving and enhancing customer service within our organization or department?

3. Do we make day-to-day decisions that are consistent with our service excellence goals?

4. Do we focus attention on both excellent customer service, as well as cost-cutting, to increase our profits and earnings?

5. Do our managers consistently demonstrate, in their everyday dealings with staff and customers, the service attitude and skills we expect our staff to show towards their customers?

What Gets Rewarded Is What Gets Done

One way to move beyond "talk" and "show" that service matters is by rewarding and recognizing your staff for service excellence. There are three important aspects of recognition:

1. A formal recognition program that is department-, division-, or company-wide and provides tangible rewards for the individual or team that best fulfills the specified service criteria.

2. Informal recognition which involves everyday acknowledgment of your staff and is often expressed by spontaneous gestures such as saying "thank you," "good job," and "well done."

3. Salary and advancement. In the final analysis, all staff have to see some personal benefit in increasing their sensitivity towards customers. If these benefits are not in some way central to the possibility of advancement in your company, then the gospel of service just becomes so much hot air.

Work Out a Working Styles Profile

When you work with someone who has a challenging work style, it's useful to sit down and strategize the best way to communicate with that person. By creating a profile, you can prepare ahead of time for difficult or important conversations such as:

- Dealing with a stressed or upset customer.
- Making a sales presentation to a tough group.
- Bringing up a conflict with a coworker.
- Presenting ideas to your busy boss.
- Meeting with a major client.
- Planning for an important event.

To begin, determine the other person's primary working style. Based on your observations, is this person more or less assertive? Do they show more or less emotional expression?

Next, what is your objective in this situation? Knowing what you want to achieve helps keep you focused on the goal and the reason you are style stepping to begin with.

Now, step back for a moment and consider the big picture. What is your working style? How about the other person's? What do your styles have in common? How are they different? Where do you think you will encounter the most friction or tension?

Plan a rapport strategy. Now that you have taken the time to assess the situation, what actions can you take to insure a better outcome? How can you best pace the other person's working style?

You want to be as specific as you can when you create this strategy. For example, if the situation is a meeting with your co-worker Kathy, and she is a People Pleaser, you might want to:

- Ask her how her day is going before you start the meeting.
- Tell her how much you appreciate all the work she does.
- Ask her what suggestions she has to solve the problem.
- Encourage her to express her feelings in the matter.
- Tell her what your feelings are, but in a passive way.
- Speak in a softer and slower tone of voice.

One caution: Don't over do it. The idea here is to get in step with the other person, not mock their style or try to turn yourself into something you're not. Style stepping is like using salt when cooking a stew: a little goes a long way.

Lastly, determine the best ways to go about communicating. As the saying goes, "Timing is everything." What would be the best time to have this conversation? Try to pick a time when you will have the other person's full attention. Where do you want to have it? Privacy may be an important issue. How do you want to have it? Is e-mail the best means, face-to-face, or over the phone?

WORKING STYLE PROFILE FORM

The working style of my customer/coworker/vendor is:

The results I want to acheive with them are:

Communication problems I have had with them in the past are:

My actions for overcoming these difficulties and achieving my objectives this time include:

Conclusion

No matter what service or product your company offers, the basis of your success is interacting with, selling to, and communicating with people. One of the most exciting, and sometimes frustrating component of these interactions, is the heart of any business—the customer. And it is the treatment of a customer that separates the excellent companies from the mediocre ones. While no business (be it a corporate giant, entrepreneurial mid-size star, or home based business) can avoid the occasional mis-step or unhappy client, they can strive to create a customer focused culture.

Becoming customer-focused involves every individual, at all levels of your organization. It often begins with an objective assessment of how customer-focused you are currently, and then identifying areas of opportunity for improving the levels of service you offer. However, for any long-term improvements in quality service to be accomplished, it is essential to involve the frontline staff in the process of making necessary changes. It is also critical that managers and supervisors demonstrate a commitment to service excellence through their own management style and actions. We hope the 60 ways presented in *Customer Service In An Instant* will help you to develop the problem solving, communication, and people skills necessary to make your goal of being customer focused a reality.

Index

About the Authors

Keith Bailey and Karen Leland are co-founders of Sterling Consulting Group, an international management consulting firm specializing in maximizing results through the people side of business. In business for 25 years they have worked with more than 150,000 executives, managers and front–line staff from a wide variety of industries including retail, transportation, hospitality, high-tech, banking and consumer goods.

Their consulting work in corporations and public speaking engagements has taken them throughout North America, Southeast Asia, Africa and Europe. Their clients have included such companies as AT&T. American Express, Apple Computer, Avis Rent A Car, Bank of America, Bristol-Myers Squibb, The British Government, DuPont, SC Johnson Wax, Lufthansa German Airlines, Microsoft and Oracle, to name a few.

In addition to their consulting work, Karen and Keith are sought after experts by the media. They have been interviewed by dozens of newspapers, magazines, television and radio stations including: *The Associated Press International*, *Time*, *Fortune*, *Newsweek*, *The New York Times*, *Entrepreneur Magazine*, *Ladies Home Journal*, *Self* magazine, *Fitness* magazine, CNN, The Today Show, and Oprah.

They are sought-after speakers and have presented for groups such as The Young Presidents Organization, The Society of Association Executives, The Society of Consumer Affairs, and The Direct Marketing Association.

Karen and Keith are the authors of five books including three editions of the bestselling *Customer Service For Dummies* (Wiley Publishing), which has sold over 200,000 copies and been translated into Spanish, German, Korean, Chinese, and Polish among others. In addition they are the authors of *Watercolor Wisdom: How Smart People Prosper in the Face of Conflict, Pressure and Change* (New Harbinger, 2006).

About Sterling Consulting Group

Sterling Consulting Group offers a variety of training programs, consulting and keynote speeches. Among the programs that SCG offers are:

The Service Advantage: a one-day customer relationship workshop for front-line staff. This program is also available as an online training program. To see a demo go to *http://www.quality-service.com/tsa/flash/demo/index.html*.

Building a Winning Quality Service Strategy: A one-day off-site for senior executives designed to facilitate them in developing a strategy for creating a more customer-focused organization.

Creating the Customer Focused Workgroup – a one day training seminar for managers on how to model, coach, reward and create an environment for quality customer service.

The Quality Service Audit: A comprehensive survey (including online, focus groups, and phone interviews) that helps a company or division identify how customer-focused they are currently and target specific areas for improvement.

Essential E-mail: A half-day training session designed to help participants improve their overall e-mail efficiency and compose messages with style and impact. This program is also available as an online training program. To see a demo go to: *http://www.quality-service.com/etraining/demo/*.

To learn more about SCG, the programs, or to book Karen or Keith to speak at your next event, please visit the Website at *www.scgtraining.com*. For any additional questions contact Karen Leland or Keith Bailey at:

Sterling Consulting Group
180 Harbor Drive #208
Sausalito, CA. 94965
(415) 331-5200
info@scgtraining.com
kbailey@scgtraining.com